GODPARENTS

Godparents

A Practical Guide for Parents and Godparents

Henry Libersat

Servant Publications
Ann Arbor, Michigan

Published by Servant Publications
P.O. Box 8617
Ann Arbor, Michigan 48107

Cover design by Michael Andaloro
Cover photo by Frank Methe

91 92 93 94 95 10 9 8 7 6 5 4 3 2 1

Printed in the United States of America

ISBN 0-89283-708-X

Library of Congress Cataloging-in-Publication Data

Libersat, Henry.
  Godparents / a practical guide for parents and godparents /
Henry Libersat.
     p. cm.
  ISBN 0-89283-708-X
  1. Sponsors. 2. Parenting–Religious aspects–Catholic Church.
  3. Libersat, Henry. I. Title.
  BV1478.R49 1991
  248.8'45—dc20   91-14205

Dedication

*This book is dedicated,
on behalf of my wife and me,
to our several godchildren,
most of whom we have sorely neglected
over these many years.
May this book be an apology and a pledge
to renew relationships.*

Contents

ACKNOWLEDGMENTS

Special thanks to those wonderful people who answered a rather lengthy questionnaire to help me do this book.

Also, I need to thank my good friend Bert Ghezzi who helped me overcome a mental block when I was asked to write *Godparents*.

David Came of Servant Publications was patient, kind, insightful, and helpful as editor of the manuscript.

My dear wife Peg, as usual, was encouraging, and she helped put me in gear when I sometimes felt my gears were stripped.

Situating the Challenge

MY GODCHILD, GAYLE MONTET, age forty-three, sat across the breakfast table from me. I had not had a serious conversation with her in more than twenty years. After her marriage and my move away from Louisiana, I had seen her only occasionally when I returned to visit my parents.

I was thrilled when, at fourteen years of age, I was asked to be godfather to the woman who now sat before me. Honestly, I didn't do a bad job of it until I got involved with college and marriage and then moved away to another state. We were part of the Cajun culture in southwest Louisiana and had strong family ties which were traditionally and culturally rooted in the Catholic faith. Being a good Catholic meant going to Mass, making those now-forgotten "Easter Duties," marrying in the church, and raising your own kids Catholic. I did those things and for awhile was closely knit to my own godparents and godchildren.

Yet Gayle's surprise visit reminded me of at least six other grown godchildren with whom I'd had even less contact since their respective baptisms. In fact, I couldn't even remember the name of one of those godchildren.

"Godparent guilt" came like a nagging voice which said, "So, Catholic deacon, editor, and author, you really have failed. You did not follow up on your promises to help your godchildren grow up Catholic. It was really a flash in the pan. How many still go to church? Only two that you know of, one in Texas and this one sitting here before you. Where are the others? Are they married and have children? Do they ever think of you? And what they must think!"

That kind of guilt is good for only one thing—to help delinquent godparents realize they have been remiss and give them the opportunity to do something about it. It is never too late to repair our relationships with God or with other people, godchildren and godparents included.

If you suffer from godparent guilt, don't panic or despair. There are godparents who succeed in establishing good relationships with their godchildren. You can, too!

Louise Primeaux of Henry, Louisiana, is one successful example whom I know. A retired teacher, she believes the godparenting role is important. She sees it as a Christian ministry, a blessing.

She commented to me, "I felt being a godparent was another way of doing God's work by helping children and their parents become good Christians. I became closer to them and to God in our prayers and bonding." She also had been asked by an adult convert to be his godmother: "He asked me to be his godmother and to teach him his prayers and prepare him to be a good Catholic. *I* was enriched."

ACUTELY FELT NEEDS

In the last two generations, American families have experienced great social change. Families no longer live in larger clans but have become dispersed throughout the United States and even the world. The emerging role of women, the effects of several wars, and rapidly developing communications and technology have added to the impact of mobility.

These social changes have had dramatic effects on family life. Among some of the needs families feel, perhaps more acutely than ever before, are the following:

• The need to feel connected, to be a vital part of a pluralistic society;

• The need to understand how faith is lived out in the world;

• The need to find new ways to build up family relationships strained by distance and generation gaps;

• The need for new skills in helping communicate faith and values to young children and teenagers;

• The need to build up and belong to smaller faith communities within the parish, such as those provided by Cursillo, Marriage Encounter, RENEW, and other adult formation programs;

• The need to develop a more meaningful prayer life.

People can find new meaning and even security by working on the relationships in which they already find themselves and by entering new relationships with a firm decision to base them on Christian values. That's why I am thrilled with the idea of stronger roles for traditional godparents and stronger relationships between parents, godparents, and children, whom I will refer to as "god-families."

I bring to this book the pain of godparent guilt, the fruit of personal reflection on this dilemma, and the decision to open communications again with my godchildren. I also bring to *Godparents* suggested aids for godparenting gleaned from the experience, frustrations, ideas, and graced insights of a number of other Catholics who kindly responded to a survey, the results of which make up a large portion of the pages that follow.

RESULTS OF THE SURVEY

I sent out thirty-one questionnaires (see appendix for sample) to people whom I judged to be serious Catholic Christians. This was not a scientific survey. Sixteen responded. Two respondents chose not to answer the questionnaire but offered some comments on their own, and a few respondents could not provide the definitive answers called for. Thus, total responses in any one category will not add up to sixteen.

When asked if they felt they had "adequate preparation to be a good godparent," four respondents said yes, and ten said no. Four who said yes attributed their preparation to their own personal faith and prayer, Catholic school education, or involvement in the charismatic renewal rather than to parish programs.

I asked them to rate themselves as godparents on a scale of 1 to 10, with 10 being "absolutely great." One chose the 8 rating; two rated themselves as 6; five rated themselves at 5; two rated themselves as 4; two gave themselves a 3; one, a 2, and one selected the 1 rating.

When asked if they ever felt any "godparent guilt," six said yes, and nine said no.

Bert Ghezzi, popular speaker and author, was rather candid in answering the question about whether he had ever experienced "guilt" or "fear" as a godparent. He said, "I don't think that the 'system' expects much, so there is no basis for fear or guilt."

Deacon Stan and Mrs. Lida Gall of Crowley, Louisiana, are parents of twelve children. The deacon and his wife, native Hollanders and naturalized citizens, said they did not feel guilty either because "it was an honor to be chosen, but only if the parents died would we have had any responsibility, maybe!"

I believe these three people are correct about the "system," but others, besides me, have also experienced guilt.

• Aurea Crawford of Maitland, Florida, an employee of a major telephone company, experienced guilt because she had lost track of some of her godchildren and because she did not have the necessary preparation to understand that godparenting is a serious commitment.

• Diane F. Brown of Clearwater, a director of Our Lady of Divine Providence House of Prayer, said, "Now that I have come to understand the true responsibility of being a godparent, I realize how I failed in my duties."

The survey asked them which of the following words best described their understanding of what a godparent should be: good example; guide; mentor; friend; teacher; substitute parent; protector of the faith.

Four respondents said they saw themselves as good examples; two, a guide; one, a mentor; one, a friend; and five, protectors of the faith.

The survey posed three attitudinal questions which asked respondents to select one of the following possible answers: strongly agree, agree, disagree, strongly disagree. The results follow:

1. Parents and godparents should have clear ground rules for dialogue and discussing tough issues. Six strongly agree; six agree; two disagree.

2. Parents and godparents should share the responsibility for the rearing of the child, particularly in faith development. Four strongly agree; five agree; seven disagree.

3. Local parishes should do more to help parents and godparents understand their roles and live up to the responsibilities they assume. Seven strongly agree, and seven agree.

Before beginning the first chapter of this book, you may want to fill in the questionnaire (see appendix) which I sent out to thirty-one people as part of my research into this topic.

After completing the book, you may want to reevaluate your answers to the questionnaire.

HOW TO USE THIS BOOK

Godparents is a handbook for parents and godparents who want to rediscover what it means to share the joys and responsibilities in the formation of young Christians.

Each chapter concludes with a *Pray, Decide, Act* program suitable for individual or group reflection and study. Each of these programs contains a reading on the content of the chapter. Some of the readings are from Scripture and some from other sources—individuals and books. The reading is followed by an opening prayer. Then individuals or groups discuss and/or reflect on the subject matter in light of their own experiences. I have included separate material *for parents* and *for godparents* in these reflections to focus issues for these two distinct audiences. This reflection is followed by an action section in which readers make a positive decision to implement some of the principles learned. Finally, there is a closing prayer asking God for strength to follow through.

I have written this book with several different groups in mind. First, I think it would be most helpful in parish baptismal classes for parents and godparents. If the godparents live far away, they could follow along in their own copy of the book and touch base with the parents from time to time, even by long-distance phone calls. This book would be helpful, too, for people who have long been godparents and want to update themselves.

Godparents could be used in other adult religious education programs in parishes. It could serve as continuing education for people who have been involved in RENEW, Cursillo, the charismatic renewal, and Marriage Encounter. For instance, couples involved in Marriage Encounter may want to use this handbook to help them in renewing or deepening their relationship with their children's godparents. The result could be a vibrant god-family which strengthens marriage and family life for all concerned.

The reflections should be approached prayerfully. Take time to read the chapters carefully and pray over the thoughts or emotions that surface. The goal is to help parents and godparents become more effective in their roles of helping young people become disciples of the Lord Jesus.

Have a wonderful time with this book. I hope and pray it will be helpful.

Deacon Henry Libersat

ONE

What's All
the Fuss about?

At best godparents are figureheads today. The responsibility for spiritual training of children rests with the parents, where this rightfully belongs. Liturgically, godparents are only welcoming young children into the Christian community as members of that community. William A. Holub, Mystic, Connecticut

BILL HOLUB, A DEAR FRIEND, brings up a real issue. Baptism is considered a community celebration. Godparents really aren't taken seriously anymore, if they ever were.

In the past, godparents were selected for two main reasons—to honor the godparent and to have someone who would help the parents keep their kids Catholic. In too many cases, the "honor" factor took precedence over the religious one.

Should we be satisfied with this attitude toward godparents? If godparents are only figureheads, why bother?

I recall one particular baptism at which I officiated as the deacon in our parish. The parents had requested that I baptize their child. They had given a lot of thought and prayer to the selection of the godparents. They had one Catholic, which is required by church law, and had a second godparent who was not a Catholic but a very committed Christian.

What I remember especially about that baptism was the level of faith on the part of both parents and godparents. The Protestant godparent (honorary sponsor is more accurate, according to church law) was a little hesitant about the value of infant baptism, but she was doing her best to be fully open to the faith of her Catholic relatives.

It was one of the most joyous moments I have ever experienced. These parents truly *expected* something great to happen to their little child. The parents realized that through baptism their child would be delivered from Original Sin that had been passed down from Adam and Eve, and they believed in all that baptism promises. They *knew* that God was claiming that baby as his own and that the child would now share in the life of God and participate in the mission of Jesus who is priest, prophet, and king. They *knew* that baptism was God's gift to us and that he could give his life to anyone—adult, teenager, or child, even to a little baby.

Four years later, as I look out from the pulpit, I see this family, and the faith is still strong. The child I baptized is growing and realizes that church and Mass are special. He was claimed by God in baptism and is being nurtured in the faith by his parents. From what I understand, both godparents are close to the child and keep in touch, remembering special days such as birthdays and his baptism day.

Baptism conveys God's intimate love and care, celebrates and makes personal the saving grace of Jesus who died on the cross for us, wipes away sin, and brings light where before there was only darkness. Baptism demands total fidelity to Jesus Christ and his Father, openness to the transforming power of the Holy Spirit, active participation in the church, and living out the faith in everyday affairs. That is a lot to expect from people, especially from a little baby, but that's why God gives babies parents and godparents as helpers.

In the Christian community, parents are primarily responsible for the Christian formation of their children. Godparents, in varying degrees, have been expected to help parents in that task. Parents and godparents, for the most part, are lay people active in the affairs of the world. Christian life and mission is lived out fully within the context of God's total kingdom which includes the world and the affairs of the world.

When Christians forget this, they amputate religion from the world, and an amputated religion is about as useful as an amputated leg or arm. If the adult Christian's faith is limited by narrow and prejudiced vision, he or she will never be able to minister to a son, daughter, or godchild effectively.

I am reminded of a man who has a very deep faith in God but regrets every minute he has to spend in secular activity. He looks upon his job as a distraction from his prayer life. He wants to spend every possible moment reading his Bible or visiting Jesus in church. He tries to impose that faith on his daughter who is young, alive, and trying to figure out how she fits into the world.

At school she is taught that she has to be deeply involved in the world. At home, by example if not by word of mouth, she is taught that the world is bad, a distraction from God. The father of the girl is divorcing religion from the world. He is not truly living his faith. He is using his faith as a crutch, as an escape from reality. He has not understood the beautiful message and mystery of God-becoming-man in Jesus Christ. He has not understood that "God so loved the world..." (Jn 3:16).

Baptism doesn't take people out of the world but sends

them into the world with the wisdom and power of Jesus Christ. People are baptized for the sake of their salvation, for the sake of the church, and for the sake of the world which God loves. Lay people are filled with a faith that calls them into the world, to love the world, and to witness in the world.

Obviously, baptism creates new relationships to help the growing Christian. Parenting and godparenting therefore have to be taken more seriously. Yet before the Second Vatican Council, parents and godparents received virtually no preparation for a child's baptism. Since Vatican II, there has been a small effort toward spiritual preparation. In many parishes, baptism preparation classes help parents understand that they are joining a parish community and have a right to expect help from the parish in rearing their children in the faith. Still these classes have the disadvantage of being only one hour long. Further, although godparents are invited, they are not required to attend. Often parents do not make the effort to include the godparents, or even update the godparents by a phone call.

Does this mean godparents are not taken seriously by the church? I hardly think that is the case, although the church is not emphasizing that role adequately at the present time.

A PRESSING NEED

There are good reasons for strengthening the role of godparents. Kathryn Slattery wrote in the January, 1990 issue of *Guideposts* magazine, "The tradition of godparenting among Christians is an ancient one going back to the days of the early church, when believers were persecuted—and when life expectancies in general were much shorter than they are today.

"While modern-day American believers are not persecuted as the early church once was, it could be said that the healthy growth and development of our children's faith is threatened as never before by the cumulative effect of society's ills: widespread divorce; broken homes; rampant materialism; both parents working out of economic necessity rather than choice; lack of parental supervision; parental mental illness; alcohol and drug abuse; parental physical, sexual, and emotional abuse; and the desensitization of our children to violence and sex via unsupervised viewing of inappropriate television, videos, and movies."

The job of Christian parenting has become more complex and demanding. If godparents are required for baptisms, then their role should go beyond formal responses in liturgies—unless, as Bill Holub says, their only role is to represent the community of faith receiving this godchild.

Godparents, however, are more than representatives of the community. During the baptismal ceremony, they are invited into the faith life of the child and pledge support of the parents in rearing the child as a Catholic. The problem is not liturgical as much as it is catechetical and practical: catechetical in that people need more instruction on the spiritual significance of godparenting; practical in that godparents do not understand they have a challenging and supportive relationship to the child.

Parents and godparents need to reflect *together* on the meaning of baptism. Many parents and godparents have been away from religious education for several years, some since their own confirmations. A great number of Catholics still regard baptism as only a religious, social function they have to go through because it is a family tradition. Others know only that baptism takes away Original Sin and makes us children of God. More in-depth spiritual instruction is needed.

On the practical side, parents and godparents need to learn more about their respective roles. At what point do godparents stop helping and begin meddling? What are some ways in which parents and godparents can develop working relationships in which prayer and faith are predominant factors?

GODPARENTS AND FAMILY RELATIONSHIPS

In our Cajun tradition, we always had a godfather (*Parrain*) and a godmother (*Marraine*), whom we called Nannan. The spouse of the godparent was also treated as a godparent, so Cajuns usually had two godfathers and two godmothers.

Recollections of my own godparents are mixed. One of my godparents is Stella Raby Morgan from Groves, Texas. To this day I call her Nan Stella—or just Nan. When I was a child, Nan was a fairy godmother who always seemed to do just the right thing at the right time. Actually, her husband was my godfather, but she took the active godparenting role rather than he. She was not only there with gifts on birthdays and Christmas, but she was there with love all year long. Nan is a first cousin, twenty years older than I, and her children are more my age and were more like first cousins when we grew up together. Her husband, Parrain Clarence, was a very busy man who was friendly and had a delightful sense of humor.

My Louisiana godfather was Adam Bourque, my dad's brother-in-law. Nannan Agnes and Parrain Adam spoke mostly French. In my early childhood, we lived in Texas and they in Louisiana—a hundred and fifty miles apart. That was considered a great distance in the 1930s and 1940s. They didn't write very often and it was not the custom to make long distance calls except on very rare occasions, so I never got to know them as well in my childhood. I remember them best from those early years for the chocolate pop they would give me when we visited their country store. I do remember, though, that to Nannan Agnes, I was also something special. When she looked at me she had that certain twinkle in her eye—and she always let me grind the coffee beans for morning coffee. In later years, when our family moved back to Louisiana, I got to know them better and our relationship strengthened.

Because we lived so close together in my childhood, I grew closer to Nan Stella. She was truly a substitute parent, a mother figure.

In our family, there was a clear understanding about what "good children" did and did not do. Any adult in the family had the right, and was expected, to correct any child when necessary. Any adult was expected to teach children right from wrong and to rush to the rescue when a child was hurt or in trouble.

Nan took her duties seriously. While my mother would spank me on occasion, Nan would not. She would correct me and tell me I had to confess to my mother when I had misbehaved. She was usually present when I faced Mama and was quick to come to my defense with something like, "But he's already apologized, Aunt Elda," and "I know he's sorry and will not do that again." Good ole Nan, making me confess and then standing by as my defender! What a wonderful memory! What a wonderful *Christian* example!

In today's society, families are even more scattered than when I was young. Few families have intergenerational relationships. Few children know their uncles and aunts intimately. Mine was the transitional generation. In my childhood, we lived as family clans, and in my adulthood the extended family is scattered all over the United States.

Maybe that's one of the reasons I didn't turn out to be such a good godparent. There were no role models for absentee *parrains* and *nannans*. However, in the Hispanic tradition, I have found a helpful model that transcends the problem of the scattered family.

Art Martinez, a Hispanic friend, is godfather to our youngest son. After the baptism, he embraced me and said, "Now I am your *compadre*." The word *compadre* means something more than *amigo*, friend, pal. Art was saying in effect, "Now, with you, I share the responsibilities for this child."

Because he was the child's *padrino* he was also my *compadre*. The two roles were, in his mind and culture, inseparable. I can't come up with an English equivalent to *compadre*, or a French one for that matter. In English, it would be something like "co-parent." However, the term is laden with spiritual and practical input for the godparent.

PRAY, DECIDE, ACT

Reading

It happened in those days that Jesus came from Nazareth of Galilee and was baptized in the Jordan by John. On coming up out of the water he saw the heavens being torn open and the Spirit, like a dove, descending upon him. And a voice came from the heavens, "You are my beloved Son; with you I am well pleased." Mk 1:9-11

Prayer

Lord Jesus, help me understand better my own baptism and how I am supposed to relate to my godchildren and their parents. Help me, Jesus, to believe with all my heart that through baptism we, too, are beloved sons and daughters of God upon whom the Spirit falls and upon whom the Father's favor rests. Amen.

Reflection

For Individuals or Groups

• If you are already a godparent, have you ever experienced "guilt"? If so, why? How do you rate yourself as a god-parent?

• In the baptisms you have attended, do you think there was adequate preparation for all involved? Did people seem to understand the meaning and demands of baptism? Was the liturgy truly community oriented, or was it pushed into a "five-minute" slot after Mass?

• Do you think there is a real need for godparents, and if so, should their roles be redefined or strengthened in any way? Discuss.

• What do you think can be done in families and in parishes to help people understand better the meaning of baptism and the role of godparenting?

For Parents

• How would you define your role and obligations as parents?

- What are your views on the role of godparents?
- How did your parents go about selecting your own godparents? What can you learn from their example?

For Godparents

- How would you define your role and obligations as godparents?
- What are your views on the role of parents?
- How is your relationship with your own godparents? What can you learn from their example?

Action

1. To prepare ourselves better for the role of Christian parent and godparent, we will:

_____

_____

_____

2. To help our parish become better at preparing parents and godparents for their roles in forming young Christians, we will:

_____

_____

_____

3. As parents and godparents, we will sit down together and discuss what each of our roles are in the child's formation:

_____

Prayer

Thank you, Lord, for inspiration and insight. Please give us, through your Holy Spirit, both wisdom and fortitude to take our roles as parents and godparents seriously. May we base our relationship on our mutual commitment to rear our children in the Catholic faith. Amen.

SUGGESTED READINGS

Boucher, John J., *Is Talking to God a Long Distance Call?: How to Hear and Understand God's Voice.* Ann Arbor, MI: Servant Publications, 1990.

Here is a catchy title for a very timely book. Sometimes people wonder whether God hears them at all or feel that it is very difficult to reach God or let him reach them. Mr. Boucher helps us learn to listen for God's voice and to recognize it—a must for anyone wanting to become a more mature, successful Christian.

Libersat, Henry, *Way, Truth & Life: Living with Jesus as Personal Savior.* Boston, MA: St. Paul Books and Media, 1989.

This book is for Catholics who want to develop a deeper, personal relationship with Jesus. It develops the themes of conversion, repentance, and discipleship along the lines of Jesus' self-description: the Way, Truth, and Life. *Way, Truth & Life"* helps Catholics share their faith with others—an aid for parents and godparents.

Schreck, Alan, *The Catholic Challenge: Why Just Being*

Catholic Isn't Enough Anymore. Ann Arbor, MI: Servant Publications, 1991.

This book gives readers a fresh look at the Second Vatican Council in an easy-to-read format, centering on faith questions that are on the minds of today's Catholics. This book will give Catholics a chance to update and renew the knowledge of their faith, helping them become more effective as Christian parents, godparents, and workers in the world.

TWO

What Does It Mean to Be a Godparent?

In thinking back, I remember one occasion when I was in church and a couple showed up to have their child baptized but did not have a godparent. I was asked to stand as the godparent. That would never happen today (I hope), but I've never forgotten that incident because of the lack of seriousness on the part of all the people involved. **Aurea Crawford, Maitland, Florida**

NOT EVERYONE APPROACHES the baptism of their children as carelessly as the parents in Aurea Crawford's story. Most people at least have selected godparents for their children. However, from pastoral experience, we know that not everyone chooses godparents for the right reasons. We also know that not all godparents are ready to assume their proper role.

What is the role of the godparent? What does it mean to be a godparent?

The answers to these questions are contained in both the baptism ceremony and in the mission to which God has called all adult Christians, namely, to be witnesses to the gospel of Jesus Christ in the world.

First, in the baptismal liturgy, the priest or deacon tells the parents: "You have asked to have your children baptized. In doing so you are accepting the responsibility of training them in the practice of the faith. It will be your duty to bring them up to keep God's commandments as Christ taught us, by loving God and our neighbor. Do you clearly understand what you are undertaking?"

The parents respond, "We do."

Then the priest or deacon turns to the godparents and asks: "Are you ready to help these parents in their duty as Christian mothers and fathers?" The expected response is, "We are."

As the ceremony progresses, parents and godparents are asked to renew their own baptismal vows, to again reject Satan and all his lies. They are asked to reaffirm their faith in the Father, Son, and Holy Spirit as one God, in the death and resurrection of Jesus, and the Catholic church. They are asked to reaffirm their belief in the communion of saints, the forgiveness of sins, and the resurrection of the dead. In other words, they are asked to declare faith in the Nicene Creed which we recite at Mass and in the Apostles Creed. It is clear from the liturgy of baptism that the church takes seriously the role of both parents and godparents in the religious formation of children.

Second, at the moment of his ascension into heaven, Jesus told his apostles and disciples that they were to go out into the entire world and spread the good news of his love and salvation. The Catholic church has always taught that part of the Christian mission of evangelization is to care for people who suffer from hunger, disease, disbelief, anxiety, and oppression.

A good Christian is one who embraces the world just as Jesus did, who becomes one with the world in all things except sin. Mother Teresa of Calcutta has captured the world's attention not because of her prayer life but because of the fruit of her prayer life. She embraces the poorest of the poor, hugs and kisses lepers, and holds the destitute dying in her arms. She is the example of what every Christian is supposed to be, a lover whose love is fed by the love of Jesus, whose arms are as big and strong as the arms of Jesus.

You and I are living in the world. Every day we meet suffering people. Every day we meet people who hate us or at least do not like us. Every day we face challenges and opportunities to preach the gospel by example, by not compromising on principle and by not saying yes to sin. Every day we are called to love with the heart of Jesus, to forgive as he does without condition, to embrace suffering for the sake of truth.

We come to grips with what it means to be Christian in our daily life, both at work and at home. Realizing this and putting it into practice is the way we can best help our children and godchildren live in the world as Christians and to embrace the world as Jesus does.

I recall one example of how a man fulfilled a godparenting role. He lived near his young adult godchild. The young man, his godchild, was beginning his own family, had dropped out of college and was now trying to make a living as a laborer. He wanted to do well for the sake of his family.

But the young man felt oppressed and depressed. He didn't understand the "macho mystique" among men on the job, the way in which adult black and white men could work side-by-side on the job and not sit together to eat lunch. He could not understand how men could live with various sorts of ridicule and other kinds of abuse.

The godfather made a lot of time for that young man. He let the young man do a lot of talking. Then he would explain that men behaved the way they did because that's the way they were taught to behave. He said, "You have to be patient and learn from them. You have to learn what to do on the job and what not to do as well. This job is hard for you, I know it is, but you can do it."

He shared examples from his own life, showed how patience and perseverance paid off in the long run. He said, "If you can learn to live with this and learn from it, if you can go through this and not become part of what you dislike so much, you'll be stronger for it—and who knows, maybe these other people will learn from you."

He was not the young man's godfather, but an uncle. In fact, I was the young man and he was my Uncle Joe. Uncle Joe's fatherly concern for me has always been an inspiration. I've found myself using his model of encouragement with young people in my own work or in our parish. He did more than help me through a difficult time—he helped me learn how to help others. In a real sense, he was a godfather to me.

Most people, because they live ordinary lives, do not consider themselves extraordinary enough to be saints or influential examples for others to follow. However, evidence abounds that God works most often through the ordinary. He calls people into ministry through other people—a parent, friend, pastor, husband, or wife. He calls people into Christian parenthood through sanctified human love and the teaching of the church. He calls people to be godparents through parents who seek support in their responsibilities.

There is no need to fear being a godparent. If you are serious about your faith and have been asked to be a godparent, in the Catholic church at least, you already have or can easily develop what it takes to be a godparent.

At the same time, if someone feels incapable of living up to the responsibilities of being a godparent, it is perfectly all right to say, "Thanks, but I simply can't for the following reasons." Refusing to be a godparent for the right reason, such as inability to fulfill the commitment, strengthens the role and heightens the profile of godparents in the Christian community.

Loretta Hobbs of Altamonte Springs, a dear friend and consultant, believes that advanced age is a good reason for respectfully declining the invitation to be godparents. "It's more than an honor," she said. "It's a responsibility. If you are advanced in years, you will most probably die just as the child really begins to sense a need for you."

She suggests that in such cases, the older people recommend that parents select younger godparents and let the elder couple stand in as *honorary* godparents. That way, she says, everybody can be happy.

Other reasons for declining the invitation to be a godparent could be any of the following: The person is already godparenting a number of children and cannot take on more; personal work and family responsibilities are too heavy; health is too poor. And there would be other legitimate reasons. Some people may feel inadequate, unprepared. This book is an attempt to show that people can become prepared. We can never forget that God supplies the grace to achieve a worthy undertaking. Catholics need to reflect on what God has already given them. Here is one of those beautiful occasions in which a "no" is a positive response.

"What it takes" to be a godparent was a free gift to you in your own baptism. "What it means" to be a godparent is something you learn from your own life experience. In other words, you are the only expert on how to live your own life in faith and goodness. Part of your job as godparent is to help your godchild live *in the world,* not escape from it, and to *live in the world* in a way that gives glory to God, helping others to live better and holier lives.

Let's look at the dynamics of faith through baptism and faith lived in the world.

FAITH THROUGH BAPTISM

As a parent and godparent, the church asks you, first of all, to be a believer. A believing Christian has a personal faith in Jesus Christ as Lord and Savior. He or she believes that Jesus founded the church on Peter and the other apostles. The believer receives, embraces, and practices that faith within the church. He or she admits the need for salvation and for forgiveness in Jesus. The believer knows that repentance, changing one's life, is the only final proof of true faith. The believer embraces the mission of Jesus which became his or her own at baptism.

The true believer wants other people to know Jesus as Lord and Savior. This is the principal reason for becoming a godparent, to share personal faith in Jesus Christ.

I remember one baptismal ceremony in which there were both strong emotional responses and deep intellectual assent to the mystery and gift of baptism. It was Holy Saturday, 1989. Following the Rite of Christian Initiation for Adults (RCIA), four adults were baptized that evening in the beautiful liturgy of the Easter Vigil, which includes the blessing of fire and water.

Our pastor baptized the adults. He poured water over their heads as they each in turn leaned over the flowing waters of our baptismal font. As each newly baptized person straightened up, he or she was greeted with thunderous voices proclaiming in song, "You have put on Christ, in him you have been baptized. Alleluia! Alleluia!"

The entire congregation had been part of the formation of

these new adult Christians. Through the RCIA process, the entire congregation had witnessed their growth in faith, their desire to become Catholics, their need for the love of this Christian community. Never before had I experienced a greater example of faith than at that Holy Saturday baptism, faith on the part of the new Christians, of the priests, and the congregation.

There, next to me, with tears of joy flowing down her cheeks, stood the mother-in-law of a new Christian, a convert from an eastern religion. Across the aisle stood the friends of a man who, born a Jew, had discovered that Jesus Christ was indeed his Messiah and Savior. In the next pew were the relatives of a person who had found the faith through her husband. There, too, were the parishioners who constituted the RCIA team. Most of all, an entire congregation of Catholics—filled with the Holy Spirit and a spirit of grateful joy to God who makes us poor humans his own sons and daughters—supported the newly-baptized members.

All of us must accept these gifts of baptism. When people are baptized as infants, they often find it helpful to go through a process of spiritual renewal, such as Cursillo or charismatic renewal, to help them consciously open themselves to the gifts God has *already given them*. It's like inheriting a million dollars when you're ten days old. If no one ever tells you about the million dollars and no one ever shows you how to put that money to work for good, you'll never be able to use it. All newly-baptized people need to be catechized and nourished.

When we were baptized, God gave us the gift of eternal life, a share in his life, the power of the Spirit to change us and transform us. I urge everyone to try to find out how he or she can learn to be more open to the Spirit. There are several good ways to pursue this; one is through involvement in the Cursillo Movement. Cursillo comes from the Spanish meaning "short course," and the weekend Cursillo is indeed a short course in Christianity, one in which men and women find deeper meaning in their faith, a clearer understanding of how present God is to them. Another good way to become more open to God's Holy Spirit is through Life in the Spirit seminars conducted by people who have been renewed in the charismatic movement. Another way is through good parish missions, novenas to the Holy Spirit, or books on the topic.

All this has much to do with godparenting, and parenting, too. God himself has called you parents and godparents to help a child grow in the knowledge and love of God, to become an advocate of justice, a lover and servant of the poor, a preacher and witness of the gospel, a lover of sinners, and an enemy of sin.

"Oh ye of little faith," Jesus once scolded his disciples. He can easily say the same thing to us when we hem and haw and try to evade our responsibilities. *You have the power! You have what you need to help your child or godchild grow in faith!*

If you are timid or uneasy about sharing your faith, even with a small child, do yourself a favor. Promise yourself to do something about it. Using this book as a reflection tool is one way to begin. Other resources are available in most parishes: adult education courses and retreats on everything from moral concerns to Scripture courses; marriage enrichment programs such as Marriage Encounter; communications seminars, and so on. If your parish does not have such programs, perhaps a neighboring one does. There are also many books available to help Catholics grow in faith so they can strengthen all their relationships as godparents and parents.

FAITH LIVED IN THE WORLD

There emerges in our own time a new call to full and fundamental discipleship in all facets of daily life. Believers are called to bridge the chasm between religion and secular life. The believer is called to love the world as the Father loves the world (Jn 3:16) and to offer his or her life for the salvation of the world, with Jesus as our motivating example.

It is not easy to find godparenting examples for this new emphasis of loving the world as part of our Christian mission. However, there are some—and there are others who, though not in godparenting roles, give a good example of what it means to embrace God's love for the world and work to make the world aware of the goodness of God.

One godparenting role stands out beautifully among respondents to my survey. Ethel Doyle of Merrick Island, New York, shares this lovely story with us.

"My first godchild became a Sister of St. Dominic in 1967. We had talked, discussed, argued, laughed, and prayed together in her younger years, and we did so again in the turbulent 1970s. She changed to the Sisters of Charity and became a remedial reading teacher and helped run a soup kitchen. When she died suddenly in 1984 at thirty-five years of age, I was shattered but joyful. She's home!"

Ethel lives life fully, and her dear goddaughter knew that. Ethel did not run away from the world, but embraced it with faith and hope. That's why her goddaughter trusted her during "the turbulent 1970s." Ethel was credible because she lived her faith in the real world and remained faithful in spite of all the negative forces that pressure people. It is that kind of faith, that basic confidence in God, that enables us to have confidence in others.

I know a cardiologist, Dr. Michael Nocero, whose fame in

his profession has spread throughout the United States. He is a dedicated physician. He sees his profession as part of his ministry in the world as a Christian. He and his wife, Mary Jo, leaders in Marriage Encounter, are two down-to-earth, delightful people. They are fully human, enjoy the good things of life, but don't let the good things own them. Mike himself prays with his own patients if they are so disposed. The Nocero couple's life is balanced beautifully between "churchy" ministries and the sense that *everything* they do is church work since they share, through their baptism, the mission of Jesus in the world. They embrace the world, love the world. They want more and more for the world. Thus their entire lives are rooted in the gospel, the Eucharist, and their family.

I know another man who lives for the sake of others. Several years ago, this man was ordained a deacon. But for many more years, he has been involved as a businessman in the welfare of his community as well.

Deacon Ed Rinderle of DeLand, Florida, sees his work as part of his ministry as a Christian. Among other things, he tries to establish a strong personal relationship with all the employees of his electronic manufacturing firm. He has regular picnics for employees and families. He himself is a strong family man. He and his wife, Mary, have reared a fine family dedicated to the service of others.

Cooperating with other business men and women of his community, Deacon Rinderle organized a special series of classes for children in school to help them learn how to apply for a job. He is part of a group of business people who help young people stay in school rather than drop out. The group promises a paid college education to students if they stay in school and maintain a B average. Members of the group meet with students as mentors on a regular basis.

Then there is Winkie LeFils of Osteen, Florida, who has been successful both in the church and in secular society. She has been president of the National Council of Catholic Women, very active in the pro-life movement, and equally active in various county and statewide farmers' organizations. She and her husband, Donald, are fifth-generation farmers who, with others in Florida, are struggling to save their farms from the "solutions" of inept bureaucrats.

These are proper role models for Christians living in the world, people who see every moment of their lives as connected to their Christian commitment. They are people whose faith truly sanctifies their own particular environments, their own marketplaces. Their faith is something dynamic which permeates all of life. They have truly, in God's name, taken dominion over medicine, family life, parish life, rural life, and industry for the sake of the kingdom of God.

If you are baptized and want to serve God and your fellow human beings, everything you do is church work. You don't have to be involved in official church ministries or in fund-raising campaigns or in parish clubs to be an active Christian. Some of us are called to *stay out* of church ministries and to become fully involved in the secular world as laborers and professionals who live their faith and convey God's love through life and labor.

God is Creator, Redeemer, and Sanctifier. When we work in love we image God the Creator. When we forgive in love, we image God the Redeemer. When we turn the mundane into a religious experience through internalized faith that finds expression in pure joy, we help sanctify the workplace and everyone in it.

Adults must convey this Christian love for the world and commitment to serving in the world to their children and godchildren. We need role models for this contemporary challenge to effective godparenting.

Aurea Crawford's and Ethel Doyle's stories provide a marked contrast to what godparenting can mean. On the one hand, it can mean nothing just as baptism meant nothing to the parents of the child Aurea sponsored; or it can mean very much, as it did for both Ethel and her niece.

If you have not had a great experience with a godparent, speak with older living relatives, especially those who came from immigrant stock, and ask them to tell you about their godparents. There are many beautiful and inspiring stories among our elderly brothers and sisters just begging to be told.

I myself remember one thing very clearly. Although I was born in Texas, our family moved back to Louisiana in 1945. My father's Parrain Paul (godfather) lived in Texas and we didn't see much of him. But when he was in Louisiana, my parents always invited the old man over for Sunday dinner. He would come, and Dad and Parrain Paul and Mama would talk about the "good old days" and catch up on the cousins in both Louisiana and Texas.

What impresses me as I think back on that relationship was the extent to which the relationship reached. Because he was Dad's Parrain Paul, he was Mama's *parrain* and mine, too. In a real sense, Parrain Paul was my grand-godfather. He loved me because I was his godson's child.

That's how seriously Cajun families took relationships in those days. If you were related to anyone in the family by blood, friendship, or faith, you were related to everyone in the family. I understand this is true to some degree among other ethnic families. Maybe it's true of the older generation in general.

I think if we can recapture that sense of kinship, we will be better able to build strong relationships in families and god-families. With a stronger sense of tradition, we will be better able to connect family and social roots. This sense of being connected with others will strengthen our faith communities, secular communities, and nation as a whole.

That's why it is so important to become rooted in the local parish, the local faith family. That "rootedness" gives us better understanding of faith and its history, places faith history in the context of family history, and helps foster a stronger and healthier sense of tradition. All this means stronger relationships and a community approach to meeting personal and community challenges.

If a Catholic immerses himself or herself into the life of a parish, loneliness or aloneness soon disappears. No one can feel like an uncharted and uninhabited island when she or he is surrounded by hundreds of loving brothers and sisters. I realize that not all parishes are vibrantly alive with the joy of the Holy Spirit. Some even appear dead. But if baptized, adult Catholics want more from their parish relationships, they need to put forth more effort. Prayer, good example, and the willingness to work are essential ingredients to help a parish come alive. So are obedience to rightful authority and teamwork, the willingness to give up personal preferences, and the willingness also to delay achieving the ultimate goal for the sake of bringing more people along on the journey toward that goal.

Actually, if we believe the parish is people and not programs, the most important thing is being together and achieving unity rather than planning together and achieving goals. The most important goal a parish can have is unity, shared life, mutual support for all parishes, compassion for the suffering, the vision of a mission to the marketplace, and special love for the poor and oppressed at home and abroad.

A vibrant and growing parish (not only in numbers but in

grace, vision, and ministry) is essential to any successful Catholic ministry, including the ministry of godparent.

If I had to choose godparents for my children today, I'd probably choose some of the same people, but for different reasons. I would not have chosen them because they are uncles or aunts or brothers or sisters who happen to be Catholic and would surely help my children if I died or left home. I'd have chosen them because they are good people whose simple faith permeates their lives from the breakfast table to the workplace to the church on Sunday.

Today, in choosing godparents for my children, I'd be inclined to bypass relatives who do not live their faith in favor of fellow parishioners who do. Whomever we chose, however, I'd do my best to see that Peg and I shared faith with them, prayed with them, created structures through which our roles would be clarified, the child's progress would be studied and evaluated, and our relationship with them as fellow disciples would grow.

After all, why ask someone to stand before God and the church to assist you in the rearing of your child if you are never going to share faith and prayer together?

PRAY, DECIDE, ACT

Reading

"You who are Israelites, hear these words. Jesus the Nazorean was a man commended to you by God with mighty deeds, wonders, and signs, which God worked through him in your midst, as you

yourselves know. This man, delivered up by the set plan and fore-knowledge of God, you killed, using lawless men to crucify him. But God raised him up, releasing him from the throes of death, be-cause it was impossible for him to be held by it.

"Therefore let the whole house of Israel know for certain that God has made him both Lord and Messiah, this Jesus whom you crucified."

Peter [said] to them, "Repent and be baptized, every one of you, in the name of Jesus Christ for the forgiveness of your sins; and you will receive the gift of the holy spirit."

Those who accepted his message were baptized, and about three thousand persons were added that day.

From Peter's discourse on Pentecost,
Acts 2:22-24, 36, 38, 41

Prayer

Lord Jesus, sometimes I am filled with doubt about my faith. I feel unworthy to be called a Christian parent, godparent, or friend. Sometimes I am so aware of my shortcomings and deficiencies that I forget how good you are to me, how much you do for me.

Help me, Lord, in this meditation, to see your goodness and generosity in every daily experience. Help me to be open to you, to look at my gifts with gratitude and my faults through your loving and forgiving eyes.

I want to be a stronger and committed disciple at home and at work. I want to be convinced of your love, of how alive you are in me and in others. I want to be a good person who will help others grow in their love for you. Amen.

For Individuals or Groups

- Do I really believe that Jesus Christ loves me enough to die for me? In what ways can I thank him for such selfless love?
- How have I been open to the Holy Spirit? How can I be more open?
- In what ways does the Spirit manifest himself in our parish community and in my family?
- What stories about my life will my friends and descendants likely pass on to the next generation?

For Parents

- Why is it so important that parents and godparents be examples of faith?
- How is this faith meant to be lived out?
- What are the implications for you in selecting godparents for your child?

For Godparents

- Can you describe your own life of faith?
- How do you seek to live out your faith in the world?
- Specifically, how can you be an example of faith to your godchild?

Action

1. God cares for us. To become more aware of all the great things God does for us each day we will:

_____

_____

_____

_____

2. To help foster stronger ties in our relationships as parents and godparents, we will:

_____

_____

_____

_____

3. To become more aware of our mission as lay Catholics in the world and the importance of loving the world and living for its redemption, we will:

_____

_____

_____

_____

4. To become more willing and able to share our vision of faith with our children and godchildren, we will:

_____

_____

_____

_____

_____

Prayer

Lord Jesus, please increase my faith. Help me to believe deeply and to be committed to my church, family, and mission in the world. Give me faith and trust in you, my God, as Father, Son, and Holy Spirit.

Jesus, help me, as I now pray the Apostles Creed, to pray it with clearer understanding and deeper conviction:

"I believe in God, the Father Almighty, Creator of heaven and earth, and in Jesus Christ, his only Son, our Lord, who was conceived of the Holy Spirit, born of the Virgin Mary, suffered under Pontius Pilate, was crucified, died, and was buried.

"He descended into hell, and on the third day, he arose again from the dead. He ascended into heaven and sits at the right hand of the Father. From thence he will come to judge the living and the dead.

"I believe in the Holy Spirit, the holy Catholic Church, the communion of saints, the forgiveness of sins, the resurrection of the body and life everlasting. Amen."

SUGGESTED READING

Droel, William L. and Pierce, Gregory Augustine, *Confident and Competent: A Challenge for the Lay Church.* Notre Dame, IN: Ave Maria Press, 1987.

In this little book of only about 100 pages, two laymen issue both encouragement and challenge to lay Catholics: Lay people are the Church in the world; they are competent and should be confident. This book is a direct mandate to be the Church in the world—a refreshing insight into what it truly means to be a Catholic lay person after Vatican II.

Libersat, Henry, *Miracle in the Marketplace: Healing and Loving in the Modern World.* Mineola, N.Y.: Resurrection Press, 1990.

Reviewers say there is a "concreteness" here, a premise that "transformation doesn't take place from the sky but through the cleansed hands and dancing feet and trained minds and focused hearts that have come to know the Lord." It is "a primer for all who are interested in the Christian vocation in the world." With its reflections at the end of each chapter, it is a help for adults who want to help young people learn to live their faith in everyday life.

THREE

Becoming a God-Family

I was godparent to some of my nieces and nephews, so there was always a close relationship as they grew up. But in today's world when so many young people leave the church, I felt powerless to interfere in the lives of those I had promised to foster the faith— so I guess I do feel guilty about this sometimes.

Today, before I accepted the role of godparent, I would make sure the family would permit me to carry out what I had promised. I would want them to permit me to have regular visits with the child to talk about the faith and instruct him or her about the importance of Jesus in daily life. **Vivian Grenon**
Altamonte Springs, Florida

N O ONE CAN REPLACE THE PARENTS OF A CHILD. No matter how strong or close the extended family or the goodness of godparents, the child's parents are still the primary educators and are held responsible by God, their neighbors, and the law for the welfare, education, and moral upbringing of their children.

When parents ask relatives or friends to help them in their responsibility of rearing their children to be good Christians, they do not lessen their own responsibility. They are merely exercising that responsibility.

THE NEED TO BE WITH COMMITTED CHRISTIANS

Children and young adults must be surrounded by committed Christians in their families, churches, and communities. If parents and godparents solidify their relationships through faith, they will benefit the child.

A good starting point would be at the baptism. The baptism of a child provides a natural, grace-filled, and teachable moment in which families can begin their journey to greater Christian commitment. They can pray together, study together, plan together, and become what I would call a *god-family*.

A god-family is a family whose true Father is God, whose elder brother is Jesus, and whose life source is the Spirit of God. I envision a god-family as one in which parents, godparents, and children all know Jesus Christ as their personal Savior and believe that he is fully alive and that his way is the best way! Can we be satisfied with less when we think of the responsibility of parents and godparents?

FOUR INGREDIENTS OF SPIRITUAL RELATIONSHIPS

There are at least four basic ingredients involved in forming solid spiritual relationships: 1) personal faith and a prayer life centered in the Eucharist, 2) fellowship, community prayer, and worship in the parish family, 3) staunch fidelity to the church and its teachings, and, 4) good, open, honest, and charitable communication.

1. Personal faith and a prayer life centered in the Eucharist. For the Catholic Christian, the Eucharist is the center of faith, because the Eucharist (the Mass) is the way Jesus gave us to be present at our own redemption. God-family relationships should be centered in the Eucharist. The baptismal liturgy should not be the last, until the godchild marries, that the godparent attends with the god-family. Worshiping together should be one of the goals set by parents and godparents as a way of growing closer together and enforcing in the mind of the child the importance and centrality of the Eucharist to our daily life.

The Mass is central to our faith because it is the way in which we step into that dramatic, heart-rending, but wonderful moment when Jesus was crucified for our sake. The Mass is not just a symbol or a celebration of what happened nearly two thousand years ago. The Mass is really Calvary made present to us in our own time. Since Jesus rose from the dead and ascended into heaven, he is eternally present to the Father. Eternity is a perpetual *now*, with no past and no future. Everything Jesus did in time, including his death on the cross, is eternally present to the Father. When we come to Mass, to the Eucharist, we plug into the eternal reality of Calvary and are present with Jesus as he hangs on the cross for us. We are also present at the Last Supper and with Mary Magdalen, Peter, and John at the empty tomb on that first Easter.

There is no greater spiritual gift to the church than the Eucharist. How many Christians go through their lives only *remembering* the price of their salvation? We, through the Mass, are actually present at our own redemption!

Faith comes with baptism. The Eucharist celebrates and nourishes that faith. It gives us great blessings, but what we receive depends in part on what we bring to Mass. Jesus will not force himself upon us. We have to be open to him, to his Spirit. We have to be people of prayer so that at Mass, the prayer of Jesus himself, we will be sensitive to the presence of God and to the power of the Spirit at work in the faith community.

We are supposed to be individually and collectively in love with Jesus. If we love him, we surely are speaking to him and listening to him and receiving his Body and Blood.

If you are a parent or godparent, or want to be, and you do not feel that your faith is strong enough, all you have to do is ask Jesus to come into your heart in a new and powerful way, to give you his Spirit, to open up your life to all those gifts that God gives so abundantly in baptism, confirmation, reconciliation, and the Eucharist.

Growth in faith will not necessarily ease your pain or your doubt or other troubles. Jesus' trust in his Father did not save him from the cross. Our faith will do more than rescue us from discomfort, it will give us the ultimate deliverance from evil. We may have to endure suffering and evil for a time, but like Jesus who had to die but was raised from the dead, we will be ultimate victors! Frequent, sincere partaking of the Eucharist is essential for this victory.

2. Fellowship, community prayer, and worship in the parish family. In Acts 2:42 St. Luke gives us a good description of how the early Christians responded to Jesus' salvation. After telling us how three thousand people were converted on the first Pentecost, he writes: "They devoted themselves to the teaching of the apostles and to the communal life, to the breaking of the bread and to the prayers."

What is clear from the outset is that the new Christians submitted to the *authoritative teachings of the apostles*, those men who had walked with Jesus and had seen him after he rose from the dead. They also had a *common life*, and this involved much more than getting together to discuss Scripture or sing hymns. They pooled their resources, helped the needy, sold their properties, and gave the proceeds to the apostles for the good of the whole church and all its members.

Their faith cost them everything. Many of them even died for their faith in Jesus Christ.

They also remained faithful to *the breaking of the bread* which was a sign of faith in Jesus Christ and the way in which Jesus was intimately present in and to the people of the community.

They further remained *faithful to the prayers*, to those traditional prayers, Jewish for them, through which they had come to know God. Theirs was a communal and a liturgical faith, not a free-wheeling form of self-satisfaction and innovation. They knew what we contemporary Christians must remind ourselves: worship is to give glory to God, not to give glory to ourselves.

If parents and godparents are to form deeply spiritual god-families, they must be faithful to the teachings of the church. They must share life and life's resources, particularly their own precious time. They must have a vibrant eucharistic faith and love for the Eucharist and all other forms of community worship, celebration, and prayer.

Remaining faithful to *the prayers* of the church is a mighty challenge. I firmly believe we need to recapture something of the Catholic piety of my parents' generation. Those related in god-families could benefit from such a rebirth. They could develop a new and fresh Catholic identity.

In the past there were the Lenten Stations of the Cross, the monthly Holy Hour, the rosary on Saturday mornings, the annual parish mission, meatless Fridays, in rural areas the blessings of the crops, and at each change of the seasons, certain Ember Days in which we were called to fast, pray, and repent.With Vatican II, we lost some of the discipline and piety which helped us identify with one another as Catholics. A return to a more rigorous piety, whatever form that would take, would help god-families to experience more deeply their catholicity and their dependence on God.

We also must be faithful to *prayer* itself. Even with help from the parish, it isn't easy to establish a prayerful relationship. Yet, if adults are serious about their faith there will be opportunities to pray with the child: during meals, giving thanks to God for gifts received, and praying for the sick. All this should be done as a natural and normal way of living.

Praying should be as natural to us as everyday conversation. Different people pray in different ways. People who are not used to praying with others realize the practice does not come easy. However, there are books of prayer offered by various publishers. Some have prayers for all sorts of special occasions—birthdays, graduations, and weddings, for example. Sometimes, sending a religious greeting card is a way to open up the avenue for prayer. Some people even decide to give Bibles or prayer books as gifts as a way to show their belief in the importance of prayer.

As previously mentioned, Catholic traditional prayers are a wonderful aid in developing prayer in relationships in all faith-communities. How wonderful it is to pray an Our Father, Hail Mary, and Glory Be. To expand our ability to pray together, before praying these traditional prayers, let each member of the god-family voice a special intention.

Dad may want to mention a co-worker whose marriage is breaking up, or a neighbor who has lost his job, or the need for God's help in considering a new job for himself, or the need for an increase in pay, or peace in the world.

Mom may want to pray for successful studies, or special help to solve differences between the children, or her employer's special needs, or a parish ministry, or the current local or national elections.

Godparents will, of course, share some of the same intentions with all adults, but they, too, should voice their own needs, even if they are the same as the parents. Godparents especially should pray for their godchildren's needs.

The children themselves will have many things to pray for—studies, sports, family relationships, friends, and special youth projects or programs. It is amazing to hear what some children come out with in prayer, amazing because we adults too often underestimate their intelligence and ability to understand. Some very young children have often voiced such intentions as "Let the war stop, Jesus," or "Please help Daddy get a job so he won't worry so much," or "Help Mommy and Daddy stop fighting."

When people are not used to praying extemporaneously, it is much easier simply to mention *intentions* before praying a formal prayer together out loud. But even mentioning the intentions in a prayerful gathering is itself *praying*.

From this simple *but genuine*, form of prayer, individuals can become more at ease and may eventually begin to pray more often in their own words. Yet even if we never go beyond the more traditional form of prayer, praying together is wonderful in any form it takes.

Some people find it difficult to pray aloud among other people. The Prayer of the Faithful at Mass has helped many people become more comfortable with prayerfully expressing their needs. Some people may never feel completely comfortable publicly expressing their needs or praying openly with others. The needs and feelings of these people must *always* be respected.

However, there are many occasions for group prayer. For

example, when parents, godparents, and children are at a little league game, why not pray for the safety of all players and for God's help that everyone play and behave well. Another opportunity for prayer is at meals, even picnics. It takes little time to thank God together for food—and this simple form of prayer reminds everyone that all good things come from God, that we all must depend on God.

When a godchild has a big event in life, it is time for the god-family to pray together. The child may be facing a test, a sports or theater try-out, an operation, the first trip to summer camp, or the godchild may be going away to college or to the armed forces—all these wonderful occasions for family prayer, occasions in which their relationship and faith are expressed and strengthened.

Godparents should be comfortable enough with prayer to be able to pray in person or on the phone with their godchildren. The ability to pray is rooted in love for people, compassion for others in pain, and willingness to share. Prayer is just one more way in which to give to others.

Prayer should not be considered something so grand that it is beyond the reach of normal mortals. Prayer is being with God, and we can all be with God. When we come together, in person, in letter, or by phone, it should be easy to share God's presence with one another. God never said we have to be spotless to pray, or that we had to be great orators. All we need in order to pray is the desire to pray, to give ourselves over to the healing and freeing power of God.

The need for prayer should be emphasized in baptism preparation classes. Prayer should be a natural part of each day, bedtime prayer and prayer before meals are good beginnings. Some godparents have helped godchildren learn their prayers and helped them prepare for their First Communion.

Here are specific examples of other possible occasions for prayerful celebration:

• When the couple discovers they are expecting, that is the moment to pray in joyful gratitude to God and to ask his protection over the pregnancy, delivery, baby, and the marriage. It is also the time to begin thinking about godparents and asking God to help in the selection of the right godparents.

Here is a suggested prayer for such an occasion: *Dear Jesus, thank you for this new life! We are so excited over our baby. We want to be good parents and to bring this child up as a good Christian. Good Jesus, please protect us all through this pregnancy, give us a healthy baby, and a safe delivery. And, Jesus, help us to find the right godparents for our child, godparents who will be serious about their responsibility to help us in rearing this child. Thank you, Lord!*

• When we ask people to be godparents, the tone of the relationship is immediately established if, after accepting the role, both parents and future godparents pray together asking God's help in their responsibilities to the child. For example: *Dear Lord, we rejoice in this new life. Help us as parents and godparents to be faithful to you, to be committed Christians who will love this child, and give him (or her) the best example possible. Bless our god-family with love. Unite us in faith and help us to learn to put you first in all concerns. Help us always, Jesus, to seek your wisdom and your will through shared prayer.*

When the baby is born, when you're preparing for the baptism, when the child cuts his or her first tooth, takes that first step, says that first word, really experiences Christmas and Easter, begins school, graduates, falls in love, fails in a class, wins a contest, becomes engaged, gets married, becomes a parent, and so on, pray!

3. Staunch fidelity to the church and its teachings. It has become almost fashionable to dissent from the official teachings of the church. Some Catholics apparently find no difficulty in approving abortion and premarital sex, to say nothing of homosexual unions.

Some people think and pray through their dissent and believe they are justified in that dissent. Others just dissent because church teachings stand in the way of their own ideas or their quest for personal gratification.

If a person feels compelled to dissent as a matter of conscience, he or she first has to understand the teaching fully, the history of its development, and the reason *why* the church teaches a particular doctrine or truth. There is a difference, too, in dissenting from defined doctrine and disciplines. For example, it would be hard to justify dissenting from the defined doctrines of the Immaculate Conception and the Assumption. These are matters of faith.

On the other hand, the rule of priestly celibacy is not a doctrine but a discipline. People can voice their disagreement from that discipline. What they cannot do, though, is disobey the church—priests cannot marry and married men cannot be ordained priests and still remain faithful to the Lord and to his church.

Parents and godparents face a tremendous responsibility in helping their young charges learn the difference between truth and popular opinion.

I never had the opportunity to discuss sexual morality with my teenage godchildren, but as a deacon in our parish, I have had several opportunities to share the church's teachings with youth. I recall one evening CCD class in which the topic of sexual morality came up.

One young fellow tried to justify the sexual activity among teenagers by saying, "But, man, everybody's doing it.

I mean, you know, it's like a natural thing to do if you really care for someone." He went on to say, "You don't know what it's like. Things are different from when you were young."

He's wrong. Not everyone is doing it—and you don't "do it" if you "really care" about someone and things are not "different" from when I was young. What is different is the social tolerance of sexual morality.

In a society which urges kids to use condoms rather than abstain from sex, when protection from disease takes precedence over moral decay, it is difficult to convince young people that God's way is the best way. "Everybody's doing it" is a hard argument to overcome, unless we adults are ourselves living good lives and can attest to happiness through observance of the commandments and the church's teachings.

There are other burning issues today—the questions of war and peace, of economic and social justice, of human rights at home and abroad. These are *all* moral questions. Godparenting takes on challenging proportions when godparents decide their role is to help parents prepare children for a Christian life *in the world,* as opposed to merely helping parents train their children to be "practicing Catholics."

To help children become well-rounded Catholics, parents and godparents have to help them understand that God's commandments are a blueprint for happiness.

God gives us commandments, not as some sort of super ego who demands obedience, but as a Father who wants his children to become fully what they can become. We are made in his image and doing his will is the best way to be more like him. Being more like God means we are more fully human, since we are made in his image. Making his way our way, his truth our truth, and his life our life is a sure formula for joy here and hereafter.

The teachings of the church are rooted in the gospel of Jesus Christ. Those teachings, in various degrees, are binding or at least strongly suggest a particular direction in our lives. To reject the teachings of the church, to assume that God's commandments no longer apply in our generation or cannot be lived without superhuman effort, is to forfeit whatever chances we have at peace and joy.

Parents and godparents, seeking to form a solid Christian alliance, must surely be obedient to the Lord and his church. How can one claim to love the Lord when one does not obey him? Jesus himself said (Jn 14:23), "Anyone who loves me will be true to my word."

Dissent, indeed, is a very serious matter. I would be a liar if I said I embrace with glee every teaching of the church. I do not. For example, I wish the church would change its teachings about mandatory celibacy for priests. I don't think mandatory celibacy is benefitting the church today. On the other hand, I would stand in strong opposition to anyone who chose to disregard the teachings of the magisterium and tried to establish a married priesthood without its approval. That is the cost of obedience if I want to be faithful as a Catholic, in spite of my own personal misgivings.

The more people share the conviction that God's way is the best way, the greater the chance for establishing order in homes, parishes, schools, and communities. It seems to me that the role of godparents is not as referee in family squabbles but as persons who share and support family and religious values.

The power of the godparent lies in the shared prayer and faith of the family, in the godparent's openness to the needs of the child, and to his or her ability to speak honestly and openly with the child, while upholding God's way and the teachings of the church. It seems to me that Ethel Doyle of

Merrick, New York, gave us a perfect example of this: She worked with her godchild through various stages of growth, listened to her worries, fears, and complaints. Ethel continued to love and to live her own faith, providing her godchild with a sympathetic ear, an understanding mind, and a compassionate heart.

Here's yet another example of a younger godparent. Kathy Byrne of Altamonte Springs, Florida, shared the following story:

"Becoming a godparent at the age of thirteen gave me a very important challenge, especially because I was a teenager. From the beginning I always felt a responsibility to be a good influence to my godchild and her sister. They lived across the street from us and looked up to me. I remember when they were in the fifth and sixth grade and wanted to quit CCD classes. I convinced them to stay in CCD by teaching the class myself. It was a very interesting and exhausting year for me because I would teach kindergarten all day, then stay late to teach sixth grade CCD in the evening. Looking back, I think I benefitted from that year as well!"

Godparents cannot be surrogate parents and should not try to circumvent parental responsibility even when parents are not as keen on faith as they might be. But godparents, by loving and supporting parents and godchild, can have a tremendous impact on the family through their own faith and faithful living. They can show forth their own personal joy in being obedient to God.

Obedience in the church and home is not a popular topic today when "rights" take on more importance than responsibilities. We hear a lot about children's rights, but very little about parental rights. For example, there are laws in this nation which deny parents the right to know their teenage daughters are going to have an abortion. In the same nation laws exist that prevent doctors from lesser interventions without parental consent. Parents must give their children consent to go on a school field day, but their consent is not required for the school to offer condoms to their children.

However, the entire question of order in society is indeed a concern for the parish family, the nuclear family, and the god-family. Obedience in the family is very important for the welfare of the children and the good of society. Parents must have authority over their children; husbands and wives must, as St. Paul directs (Eph 5:21 ff), submit to one another, live for one another in the Lord. Love is a decision to do what is best for the beloved. Nothing can be more important to a beloved than eternal life. If we love, we will help our loved ones live according to God's way. As it says in Romans 13:9-10: "The commandments, 'You shall not commit adultery; you shall not kill; you shall not steal; you shall not covet,' and whatever other commandment there may be, are summed up in this saying, [namely] 'You shall love your neighbor as yourself.' Love never does evil to the neighbor; hence love is the fulfillment of the law."

This kind of love must begin with husband and wife and be lavished on their children. Godparents connected with the family must give and receive this love, the love that does no wrong, the love that is obedient to God and the church.

4. Good, open, honest communication. Communication is one of the most essential elements in any relationship. Without communication, relationships will never develop. Even strong relationships can be destroyed when communication breaks down.

Every family, with a little thought, can come up with examples of how good communication could have prevented misunderstandings and hurt feelings.

Let's examine a family scenario in which lack of communication resulted in injustice and hurt feelings.

George, fifteen, was going with some friends to the nearby irrigation canal for a swim. Joe, his seven-year-old brother, although he couldn't swim, wanted to tag along.

Their mother gave Joe permission to go, but said he was not allowed in the water at all. So Joe, wearing his swimsuit, sat on the canal bank, watching the others. George urged Joe to come into the water. Joe refused, reminding George that "Mother said no."

George pulled Joe into the water and tried to teach him pointers about swimming, but the younger boy kept protesting, "Mother said no." After George put Joe back on the bank, the younger brother ran home. His mother took one look at him, knew he had been in the water and meted out a punishment before he could say, "But Mama, George made me do it." George came in later and laughed at Joe, and laughed even more as Joe slipped into an impotent rage.

About two days later, Joe had come in for supper in filthy hands and went to the bathroom to wash up. He didn't wash his hands off enough and left big dirt stains on his mother's beautiful white "company towel." Later, Mother saw George coming out of the bathroom, discovered the dirty towel and blamed him. She scolded him thoroughly in spite of his repeated claims of innocence. Joe realized that the Christian thing to do would have been to confess and save his innocent brother, but revenge was too sweet a temptation. Joe enjoyed the last laugh.

If this family had established good communication, Mother would have made sure George knew he was responsible for his younger brother—or she would not have imposed this responsibility on George; George may have really listened to Joe's protests as he dragged him into the canal;

Mother may have listened to Joe's squeals of protest as she punished him; Joe would have admitted soiling Mother's towel. Because this family did not have a good communication system going, all three people—Mother, George, and Joe treated others unfairly.

In our own marriage, Peg and I had a lot to learn about communication. Marriage preparation for us involved one session with the parish priest. There were no Pre-Cana conferences, no classes on building relationships or on good communication.

We simply entered marriage and faced the inevitable problems without adequate preparation. Had we not loved one another so deeply, our marriage may well have failed.

It took years for us to understand the dynamics of our different personalities, to understand that we didn't have to like the same things and the same people to have a good time. One major problem was deciding how to rear the children. Another was agreeing on the kinds of friends we should have. Still another was management of family finances and another was how to resolve differences. Today we are working with people preparing for marriage, and we can see how much better it would have been for us if we had been taught to understand the issues and to resolve them through skilled communication.

Let's review some basics of successful communication.

• Christian communication is always motivated by love. Businesses may have excellent communication systems. Too often business communication is motivated primarily by profit motives and secondarily by some humanitarian impulse to help people live fuller lives. Christian communication is motivated by the desire to want and do what is best for the beloved.

Among Christians, what is best for the beloved is total

conformity to God's will, eternal life, and peace of mind, heart, and soul. If everyone in the family wants what is best for all the beloved, you will have a family filled with grace, peace, and joy.

• Honesty and charity are "siamese twins" in communication between Christians. You can't have one without the other. Jesus, in communicating with the woman at the well (see Jn 4:4 ff), was gentle and loving. He did not put on a face of divine wrath and accuse her of adultery. Rather he led her gently to face herself. As she encountered the truth about herself in the light of his love, she was moved in one instant from sin to evangelization. She accepted Jesus and ran off to tell her whole town that she had found the Messiah.

Jesus did not forsake truth and honesty for the sake of love. Rather, he shows us that love and truth go hand-in-hand.

• People have to agree to set up ground rules for communication. Good will is not enough. We have to use our heads in communicating.

For example, the best time for family members to communicate with me on serious matters is Saturday morning or Sunday after Mass. My weekdays are generally filled with stress, so I am naturally not delighted to have more stress dumped on me at such times. But weekends are less stressful and are more or less reserved for family and fun. I am naturally more open on weekends.

If parents and godparents are interested in developing good communication, they have to agree on when is the best time to communicate.

• Communication is a big challenge to many people because it means, basically, being open and vulnerable to others. We all need help in beginning to communicate with one another.

For parents and godparents, it may be helpful to begin with discussion of the date of baptism and where the reception will be held after the baptism. Also, early on, even before the baby is born, they may want to discuss how they will celebrate the baby's birthdays, first words, first steps, first tooth, first day in pre-school, and so on.

These are really simple matters, but in discussing them, parents and godparents have already established the fact that they *can and do communicate.* From that point, it would be easier to discuss the more sensitive and important concerns, such as the role godparents will play in helping the parents in the religious formation of the child.

• In communicating with others, our thoughts, values, and suggestions must be stated clearly and carefully. When there is a disagreement, especially where there is a serious disagreement, never imply bad motives to those with whom you disagree.

Psychologists have developed some very helpful insights into human personality traits. People think differently. They resolve questions differently. People also operate at different levels of maturity.

Much of what we know about the maturing process in people comes from the work of three great thinkers: Jean Piaget, a Swiss scientist, who recorded the development of children from infancy through puberty; Lawrence Kohlberg, a psychiatrist at Harvard's Graduate School of Education; and James W. Fowler, a researcher in faith development.

Their work is vast. Mary W. Wilcox, a graduate of the Iliff School of Theology in Colorado, wrote a book in 1979 that brings together the findings of these three men and those of many other people in the field. *Developmental Journey,* listed in the "Suggested Reading" at the end of this chapter, is used in schools of ministry.

Risking an injustice to the work of these scientists, I would like to very briefly allude to part of their findings as follows:

People achieve different levels of moral maturity and make the right decisions for different reasons. One person (child or adult) makes a moral decision (e.g., to obey a rule or law) for fear of punishment; another, for the expected reward; another, for the perk of praise; still another, because it is one's "duty" to do what is right; finally, a person may make a moral decision because of personal conviction that it is right to do so without much thought of reward, punishment, perks, or duty.

Understanding these responses makes it easier to communicate with one another—particularly when working with a growing, developing child. It is sometimes harder for adults, in dealing with one another, to recognize these different stages of moral reasoning. Yet understanding *why* a person makes a decision can be as important as the decision itself.

People also gather information differently and make decisions differently. For example, I have worked with people who never seem to be able to make a decision. We collect data, think, and pray. Then when I am ready to make a decision, they balk, insisting that maybe more thought and facts are needed.

In every family, parish, or work force, decision-making is affected by these and other factors. For example, I am a person who gathers facts intuitively, and I want to make a decision "yesterday." I can walk into a room and sense the unanimity or tension, excitement or apathy. Others may walk into the same room and not immediately "see" what I see. They have to see and hear and weigh and compare to make a decision. My way is not better than their way, it is just different.

When we became more aware of these differences in our

office through the Myers-Briggs personality profile exercise, we were able to appreciate one another's gifts and to understand why we responded differently to the same situations. (See "Resource" at the end of the "Suggested Readings" following this chapter.) We began to rely on one another more, some trusting my intuition when there was little time for assimilation of facts, and me trusting more the hesitancy of others when it came to making decisions. We learned that we complemented one another in beautiful and effective ways.

In just about every area of the country, in almost every diocese, there is probably someone well-versed in the Myers-Briggs instrument and in stages in moral growth. Workshops can be developed for special groups—such as parents and godparents preparing for baptism. I strongly recommend workshops along these lines to develop communication skills.

• Listening is perhaps more than half of communication. Listening involves more than hearing. *Listening* implies understanding. To foster understanding, it might be helpful for everyone to agree to a period of quiet reflection after ideas have been exchanged. This quiet time will give everyone a chance to reflect more carefully on what has been shared. This will help everyone *listen* better.

• Try to find the common denominator. Between parents and godparents, it may well be love and concern for the children. Build on that common ground. Once people agree on their common ground and objectives, it is easier to arrive at a consensus for action.

The common denominator between adults and children is not always quickly apparent, especially when small children are concerned. Adults will have to use their imaginations to establish a common ground with children. They will have to become like little children. They will have to speak the language of wonder and simplicity. Parents and godparents, where younger children are concerned, will have to rediscover mud pies and butterflies.

Becoming like a little child is wonderful therapy. The times I can be alone with some of my little grandchildren are precious. I love to tell them stories, both standard fairy tales and some my own grandfather passed on to me. To be with little children as they discover flowers, birds, puppy dogs, and bunny rabbits is to rediscover the wonders of creation. No wonder Jesus told us to become like little children. Little children are so open to beauty and mystery. Beauty, to the child, is pure experience; mystery, intimacy with adventure.

• Prayer is essential in Christian communication. When people call God to witness their conversations, when they openly accept Jesus into their midst, they have accepted the source of all love and holy power. What an atmosphere for Christian communication!

There are a couple of very simple statements about prayer that have helped me over the years. Both were made by Mother Angelica of Eternal Word Television Network, Birmingham, Alabama.

The first one is, "The best way to pray is the way you pray best." Some people pray better kneeling; others, sitting; others, walking in the woods. Prayer is very personal. It should feel comfortable. While inspired and motivated by the Holy Spirit himself, prayer is also fully human and flows from the heart, mind, soul, and body of the person praying.

The second statement is, "Prayer is not something you say or do; it is being with Someone." Prayer is communion, something beyond even the best of communication. Prayer is being present to God and letting God be present to you. When we pray together, we are asking God to mold us into his heart and mind, as a god-family.

In god-families, God has something to say about our relationships, our guidance of the children in our family, our relationship to the entire church, and our role in the world. How well we listen in prayer determines how well we will communicate with one another and fulfill our responsibilities as parents and godparents.

Pray, Decide, Act

Reading

"Again I tell you, if two of you join your voices on earth to pray for anything whatever, it shall be granted you by my Father in heaven. Where two or three are gathered in my name, there I am in their midst." Mt 18:19-20

Prayer

It is difficult, Jesus, to form deep relationships based on prayer. So much in our lives draws us apart and fills our minds with distractions, lies, and half-truths. We are told we should be rugged individualists, that we should be able to make it on our own. But that's not how you made us, Lord. You made us to be a people who love and support one another. No wonder, Jesus, there are many people suffering from emotional disturbances! We are trying to be something we are not.

Lord, please give us a sense of holy dependence on you,

our source of life and unity. Heal us of all division, and give us the grace of your Spirit to become one in mind, heart, and soul, especially in all our Christian relationships. Amen.

Reflection

For Individuals or Groups

• Have you ever experienced what it means to be part of an extended family with your grandparents, uncles, and aunts living close by and sharing life's joys and sorrows? If so, what did that experience mean to you? If not, have you ever "adopted" an extended family, regarding others as brothers, sisters, uncles, aunts, and so on?

• Do you believe parents and godparents should have a special relationship, such as that proposed in the concept of a "god-family"?

• We have often been told that the Eucharist is the center of our Catholic faith. What does this mean to you?

• Which of the church's teachings do you have most trouble accepting? Why do you find it hard to accept?

• Are you able to communicate openly and honestly with those you love?

• Do you find it hard or easy to pray with others?

For Parents

• How could your parish help you in rearing your children? Are there needs which present parish programs do not meet? Which programs at present are helping you become the kind of parent you want to be?

- Please try to name a few things which your children's godparents could do to help with the rearing of your children.
- If you are hesitant to ask your children's godparents for help, you may want to explore why.

For Godparents

- What do you want and expect most of all from (1) the church, (2) the parents of the child?
- When you consider the areas covered in this chapter and your own areas of strength as a Christian, how could you best support your god-family?
- How can you be supportive of your godchild's parents and really get involved in your god-family without undermining parental authority?

Action

1. To determine the boundaries of our relationship as parents and godparents, we must discuss and decide on the following concerns:

_____

_____

_____

2. To commit ourselves to these discussions, we agree now to the following schedule of meetings:

_____

_____

_____

3. To help other parents and godparents in our parish, we will suggest the following ideas to our pastor and director of religious education:

_____

_____

_____

Prayer

Help us, Lord, to be open to one another, to the promptings of your Spirit and to all the opportunities we have to serve you. Let us learn to share our ideas in a spirit of openness and trust. Help us to learn to trust your intervention in our lives as we ask you to guide us and help us. Amen.

SUGGESTED READING

Ghezzi, Bert, *Becoming More Like Jesus: Growth in the Spirit.* Huntington, IN: Our Sunday Visitor Press, 1987.

Bert Ghezzi is one of the best popular Catholic writers. In this little treasure, he helps focus on the "fruit of the Spirit" in Jesus' life and leads us in prayerful reflection on how the Holy Spirit works in our own lives. This book has been one of Mr. Ghezzi's most read works.

Knight, David, *The Good News About Sex.* Cincinnati, OH: St. Anthony Messenger Press, 1979.

Father Knight, a popular retreat director and writer, has provided Christians with a good handbook on human sexuality. Readers will discover that sex is indeed good news. Sex "does have meaning and value, and our Christian tradition has much to say (about sex) even though we often do a poor job of explaining it," Father Knight says. This book will be very helpful for parents and godparents helping shape Christian sexual values in the young.

Scanlan, Michael, *Let the Fire Fall.* Ann Arbor, MI: Servant Publications, 1986.

Father Scanlan's book is really a moving and inspiring story about his own personal conversion, written in a way that inspires the reader to ever deeper conversion. Father Scanlan's story of his reconciliation with his step-father is a powerful aid to anyone who wants to learn how to love and forgive—two inseparable ingredients essential to Christian life in the home, family, god-family, and marketplace.

Wilcox, Mary M., *Developmental Journey: A Guide to the Development of Logical and Moral Reasoning and Social Perspective.* Nashville, TN: Abingdon, 1979.

A scholarly, readable work, *Developmental Journey* compiles the findings of major thinkers in the area of moral, logical, and faith development. This is a valuable book for parish adult education programs which seek to enable adults to work with children and with other adults in relationships which are the fabric of daily life.

RESOURCE

The *Myers-Briggs* instrument in personality evaluation was developed by Isabel Briggs-Myers and published by Consulting Psychologists Press, Inc. in Palo Alto, CA, 1976. The instrument is administered only by trained personnel. Interested parties may contact their local director of religious education, diocesan Catholic Charities, or family life counselors, as well as local universities.

FOUR

Making God Visible

Christ is a sacrament because he incarnates God and reveals him. "He who sees me sees the Father" (Jn 14:9). Incarnation and sacrament are the same idea: an invisible reality finds a visible embodiment, and what is transcendent comes to us in matter. God is the great mystery beyond our grasp; in Christ, we touch him. We hear his word, feel his care, experience his faithfulness, know his compassion and mercy....

Next comes the church.... The church is the community of all those persons who belong to Christ.... Like Christ, Christians incarnate something and bring it to visibility. What we incarnate is Christ, and that is why we are called the body of Christ. For Jesus of Nazareth is no longer present as an individual on the stage of history, as he was for a limited period of time in the first century. He died, and has undergone transformation into a glorified state. His incarnation in the world now is the church, all those human beings who have been baptized into him and breathe his Spirit. Thomas N. Hart

The Art of Christian Listening, **Paulist Press**

I HAVE A GREAT PROBLEM WITH CERTAIN PREACHERS who teach that God will give you anything if you just ask for it in the name of Jesus. Evidence abounds that God has better sense than to grant our every whim. In fact, evidence abounds that

77

he will sometimes not grant every serious and seemingly worthy request, for his wisdom and love are infinite, perfect, and pure. He knows better than we do what we truly need. Only he knows what good can come from situations which seem totally senseless and without any redeeming value.

There is one certainty about God answering prayer: If you want to grow closer to God, if you want to be holy, if you want to live according to God's will, that *is* a prayer he will answer! If you want to be able to share your faith and are willing to live it and ask for God's help in learning how he intends *you* to share *your* faith, that too is a prayer God will answer.

I personally believe many godparents suffer "godparent guilt" because they feel that they cannot live up to their commitment and do not know how to begin to grow and become more effective faith-sharers.

There are four basic principles which can help Christians experience freedom from fear or feelings of inadequacy in living and sharing their faith. The four principles follow:

1. God is *in* us, and he makes himself visible in us and through us;

2. A living faith is a relationship with God;

3. A living faith is itself a proclamation of the gospel;

4. The ultimate word of faith is love.

Let's take a brief look at each of these principles.

1. GOD IS IN US

God is with us and in us. He is in all things. All people and all creatures of God are sacred because they find their origin and completion in him. He made us and all things and said that everything was good.

Unlike the "bad news" preached by the New Age Movement, however, Christians do not believe everything is God. A New Ager has no problem moving from God-is-in-me to I-am-God. This New Age is, to me, a new expression of paganism, of idolatry, of the sin of pride and arrogance.

We are made in God's image; not he in ours. He is almighty, everlasting, good, holy, omnipotent. He is life itself, love itself. He is eternal. That God, pure spirit without limits, would become one of us, fleshly and very limited, is the most baffling mystery proclaimed by Christianity and the most profound sign of his limitless love for those who even fail to love him back.

Not only did he become one of us and die for us, since his resurrection, he has again put on our flesh. As Thomas N. Hart states in the above quotation, Jesus is incarnate in us. He makes himself visible in us. In Jesus of Nazareth, people were able to see, hear, and touch the transcendent God. Now in us, people see, hear, and touch that same glorified Jesus of Nazareth.

Jesus is in you. His Spirit transforms you into his image. Others see Christ in you.

Any baptized Christian can say with St. Paul, "… the life I live now is not my own; Christ is living in me. I still live my human life, but it is a life of faith in the Son of God, who loved me and gave himself for me" (Gal 2:20).

What does that mean? How can that be?

I have often shared my own story in person and in print. Here, I will share more briefly, just to encourage everyone to believe that we can indeed grow in knowledge and love of God, that God really cares for each of us, and that he stands ready to help us when we ask for help in growing in our love for him.

Many years ago I was an unhappy man. I believed in God,

was working for the church, had a loving wife, and wonderful, loving children. I went to Mass and communion. I prayed as best I could. But I was still unhappy. I felt unloved.

One day I managed to have a meeting with Sister Briege, a nun with a teaching and healing ministry, whose headquarters are in Palm Harbour, Florida.

I told Sister Briege that I really wanted to love God and to get to know him better. She told me that as a teacher she had great difficulty winning the confidence of first-graders, even though she loved them and hugged and kissed them. She said to me, "How hard it must be for you to trust a God whom you've never seen."

As she prayed with me, she mentioned two situations that were deeply troubling me. I had not told her about the people involved who had hurt me so deeply. As she mentioned the broken relationships, I was overwhelmed with the presence of Jesus. I understood that God had put that information in her mouth so I could at last be sure that he knew me, understood me, and loved me. I wept for a long time.

My life was transformed in those few minutes of prayer. I experienced deep psychological healing. My heart opened up to God, and I was able to believe with all my strength that he lived in me.

I still had to struggle with daily life, there were still broken relationships, inadequate family finances, my quick temper, and the tendency to sin. Only now it was different. I knew Jesus Christ personally, and he filled my life.

Fourteen years later I still struggle and sin, but I feel Jesus' presence in my life. I am stronger today than I was before Jesus touched me through Sister Briege's prayer. Once you have felt the love of Jesus, once you become convinced of his love, your problems may not vanish, but you see them in clearer perspective. Your sense of inadequacy may not go away, but you'll find that holiness is surely possible without great intellectual sophistication. You'll discover with great joy that holiness is possible for all of us and it gives witness to our God.

Jesus is real. He wants to be a conscious part of your life. He wants you to know him and to experience his love in your life. And he wants you to be able to share that love with your children and godchildren.

2. A LIVING FAITH IS A RELATIONSHIP WITH GOD

I remember watching the television news one night. There was a story about a storm or a flood. Many people had died. The newscaster was interviewing a middle-aged woman who had lost a dear relative in the disaster. The bereaved woman said something like this: "I can't understand why the Lord took him now. He was so young. But I know one thing. The Lord knows what is best, and I must try to see all this through his eyes."

When a tornado crushed my maternal grandparents' little home, killing Grandpa and critically injuring Grandma, I remember Grandma saying something she always said in times of confusion or trouble, "Well, in God we trust."

Trusting God is a sure sign of faith, an element of holiness. It isn't really fashionable these days to talk about holiness. Holiness is considered weakness. Some good Christians mistakenly believe that to desire holiness is prideful and a sure sign we are not holy. That is unfortunate, for Jesus said we must be holy as his heavenly Father is holy.

That's a tall order if we try to do it ourselves. The secret to holiness, however, is to embrace the gift of faith given at baptism.

Faith is not something we do. It is not primarily the process of believing or even the *belief* that there is a God who is Father, Son, and Holy Spirit.

Faith is the gift of *knowing* God, not only knowing that he exists. Faith is knowing God personally from his revelation of himself to us through Scripture and his church. To have faith and to be faithful is to live with God in the nitty-gritty of everyday life. The only way to be capable of this is to have a personal relationship with Jesus, to make Jesus the center and driving force of our lives.

"I am the Way, the Truth and the Life," Jesus tells us (Jn 14:6). Even though he is now glorified in heaven, he is alive in us. We discover the Way, Truth, and Life in our own hearts and minds and spirits as we turn to him and worship him. Since Jesus is in paradise and he is in us, we already are beginning to experience everlasting life!

You cannot "live the faith" if you do not have a *living faith*. A living faith is not external adherence to laws and disciplines. Nor is it only an intellectual nod to the humanity and divinity of Jesus and his saving life and death. A *living faith* is a love affair with Jesus whom you know to be alive and glorified.

As a Christian grows in living faith, he or she begins to speak to Jesus intimately. Prayer is no longer a formal and dry experience, but a warm and intimate encounter with a friend and brother who is also God and Savior. Isn't this what we want, not only for ourselves, but for our children and godchildren as well? Should we settle for anything less?

I have a dear friend, an ordinary businessman, who several years ago was afraid his business would fail. He worked hard but could not increase sales. One time driving home from a fruitless day trying to sell orders for his manufacturing firm, he was so discouraged he pulled his truck off to the side of the road and stopped.

He said, "God, if you're real, you'll have to show me. I want to believe, but I'm so snowed under with problems, it seems to me that you're not really there."

Suddenly, he said, his truck was filled with the presence of God. He sensed Jesus sitting next to him. He tells the story often of how he just sat there, talking with Jesus, his friend and Savior. My friend's life was changed. To this day, Jesus is real and present as an intimate friend in his life and the life of his family.

You don't have to feel inadequate when it comes to living and sharing your faith. If your prayer is for holiness, for a deeper and more faith-filled relationship with Jesus, your prayer *will be answered*. God loves you and wants you to know he loves you. He appreciates your love and friendship.

I recommend two things to help people grow in faith-based relationships. First, prayerfully read the Scriptures. If you choose one Gospel or epistle, and read just a little of it every day, you will begin to see how your relationship with Jesus grows.

As part of that discipline, it is a good idea also to share your insights into the Scriptures with your god-family, especially at those times when you gather to pray and reflect on your relationships with each other.

Second, work consciously to develop a Eucharist-centered faith. When you come to Mass, try to remember that you are, in a special way, in the presence of the living Jesus Christ, the same Jesus who walked the earth loving and teaching and healing so many years ago. Try to develop a conscious appreciation for Jesus in the Eucharist. As you receive him at Communion, pour out your praises, gratitude, and needs to him in that most wonderfully intimate moment.

3. LIVING FAITH PROCLAIMS THE GOSPEL

If you are intimate with God, you *will* share your faith. Maybe you won't preach or teach formally, maybe you won't feel comfortable "talking religion," but if you are intimate with God, he will use you to speak to other people. You will "conduct" God in much the same way a copper wire conducts electricity.

Friends of mine, Paul and Justine Devlin, once said: "God's work is always veiled to those who desire to do his will. We can only hope that our influence encourages our godchildren's faith walk."

Another friend, Gladys Bertram of Altamonte Springs, also shared some thoughts in this regard. When one of her godchildren was a teenage girl, Gladys often spent weekends with her. "At those times, she would ask me questions about God and his saints—questions she would not ask her parents. She was always curious about my faith and what *I* believed. There were times when we talked until three in the morning.

"One of the challenges I experienced with my godchild on those weekends was convincing her that God loved her, that she was truly a beautiful and intelligent young lady, and that God had a wonderful plan for her life. Being a godparent not only includes witnessing for Christ, but also repeatedly reassuring and affirming a godchild."

Part of the tension of being a good parent or godparent is never really knowing whether *what* we are doing or saying is the best thing to do or say. Yet if we have a deep, faith-filled relationship with God, we can handle the tension and the uncertainty.

I am weak. I sin. I need forgiveness. I need God's wisdom and all his gifts. Because I am so needy, as long as I am open to God, God can use me still to help other people see him, feel him, and experience his love.

St. Paul said he would boast only of his weaknesses, because when he was weak, it was then that he was strong (see 2 Cor 12:9-10). We have to believe as Paul believes. It may sound foolish to people without faith, but to the faithful, Paul's confidence in God's strength within his own weakness is believable and cause for great joy.

I am reminded of the story of the five loaves and two fishes (Mk 6:34-44). There was a great and hungry crowd far from town. Jesus took what his disciples had, only five loaves of bread and two small fish, and made it more than enough for a crowd of several thousand!

That's what Jesus promises to do for us parents and god-parents if we give, in faith, what little we have. He can take our small faith and limited understanding and make it more than enough, through his presence in us and our relationships, to do what he wants done.

I am reminded of my wife's dear grandmother. "Gam" was completely illiterate. She knew so little about her Catholic faith, but she was a holy woman and left a legacy of love and faith in her wake. My wife recalls that it was Gam who, in spite of her bulk and arthritic condition, walked with her the two miles to church for catechism and helped her learn her prayers.

Gam was a woman of deep prayer, and her heart was filled with love, a heart as big as her Cajun sense of humor and her appetite for life and all of life's blessings. She could not explain theology. She couldn't read or quote Scripture, but she was a living gospel. She had no master's degree in religious studies, but she had a loving relationship with the Master and was ready to let him work in and through her.

One of the best ways to become a living gospel is to develop an attitude of grateful repentance, grateful because God redeemed us, and repentant because such a love demands a positive response from us.

I often sit in our parish church and gaze on the life-sized crucifix which towers in our sanctuary. I look upon the image of the body of Jesus, nailed to the cross. I reflect on his suffering, on his willingness to undergo this terrible, unjust death for my sake. I reflect on how he must have felt like a failure and the terrible psychological pain of being hated and unjustly condemned.

Such reflection always makes me grateful that God who is so just is also so loving. He loved me and all of us enough to send his only Son to die in our place, to redeem us and bring us to life everlasting. What great love that is!

This awareness of God's love and his holiness makes me want to change my ways, to repent of pettiness and whatever sins seem to plague me. I *want* to change as a response to God's love and as a sign of my love for him.

Concentrating on his love and trying to live a better life, I can become more loving and tolerant, more understanding—in a word, more Christlike. I can become a person whose living faith proclaims at least a little of the gospel of the Lord.

Through the centuries, meditating on the passion and death of Jesus has turned great sinners into great saints. It will help us, too, to become living gospels of the Lord. That's the kind of witness that will really make a difference in the lives of our children and godchildren as well.

4. LOVE—THE ULTIMATE WORD OF FAITH

The late Penny Lernoux, herself a controversial Catholic writer, shared a moving story in one of her books, *People of*

God. The story was about Catholics in Nicaragua who suffered terribly for their faith.

One evening in the village of Santa Cruz, the military came in and threatened to wipe out the village the next morning unless all five village catechists were executed by the villagers. The military said that relatives of the catechists had to be the executioners.

That night, the villagers all said they would die rather than execute their beloved catechists. That is, all said this except the five catechists. The catechists said it was better for them to die rather than entire village. So, the next morning, everyone went out of the village to a site where five new graves had been dug, and relatives of the catechists killed them with machetes.

This story is very troubling. The military was cruel and unjust, the people of the village and the five catechists were brave. The relatives—turned executioners—were especially brave. It is a horror story hard to believe for us North Americans who more often than not, on a typical morning, have to struggle with such difficult decisions as choosing between cereal or bacon and eggs, selecting what to wear to work, or fussing with spoiled children who don't want to go to school.

Love is the ultimate word of faith, the ultimate expression of faith, the ultimate proof of faith. Thanks be to God that we do not all have to make such gruesome decisions. But we all make decisions every day. Every day we choose between ourselves and others.

The greatest legacy we can leave is love. We are blessed indeed when, in thinking of us, people think of a living and lively love.

Some of my heroes are real sinners. For example, a woman I will never meet was the subject of a special feature carried by the Catholic News Service some years ago. The feature appeared in various Catholic papers around the country.

The heroine of the story was a practicing prostitute, who on the down side of fifty, discovered that she had wasted her life. She wanted to rescue young girls who were trapped in prostitution, but all she knew was prostitution. So she continued to ply her trade, using the funds to help young girls escape to a better life.

We can never condone the sin, but in this case it is very easy to admire and respect the sinner—and yes, to love her as a sister who loves, in one way at least, as Jesus loves. Her story reminds me that St. Paul himself once said that as much as he yearned to be in heaven, he gladly remained on earth for the sake of those who depended on him to learn about Jesus (see Phil 1:21 ff).

Think of Jesus hanging on the cross. Everything about his passion and death pointed to failure. He had preached love and he was hated; he had preached forgiveness and he was condemned; he had preached fidelity and his closest follower denied and deserted him; he had preached salvation and he was condemned.

Yet suffering the agony of a scourging and a crown of thorns, his hands and feet pierced with terrible nails, his body's weight dragging against his wounds, his lungs gasping for breath and filling with fluid—in all this, Jesus, as a human being, could raise his eyes to his Father and respond as his Father directed him to: "Father, forgive them, for they do not know what they are doing." While Jesus is also fully divine, here we see the full meaning of his suffering for humanity.

Love is the ultimate word of faith. When we say "Jesus" we have said "love" and "faith."

As parents and godparents, we must pray and strive to love like that. Particularly in dealing with children, we must reflect the gentle healer who is Jesus and the loving forgiver who is the Father. We have the strength to do this because we ourselves are baptized and Jesus lives in us.

Most of us love with a holy love every day but simply don't realize that we do. We love as Jesus loves when, dreading another boring or taxing day on the job, we go to work for our family's sake. We love as Jesus loves when we sit up with sick children, or take time out for PTA meetings and ball games and catechism instructions. We love as Jesus loves when we comfort grieving people or help teenagers cope with their growing pains and new physical urges.

Some Christians find it difficult to believe that their love actually mirrors God's love. They feel ineffective and unproductive. Their sins weigh them down. Their "ignorance" about God makes them tongue-tied when it comes to praying in public or giving thanks to God or sharing their faith even with a little child.

I'd like to recommend a little spiritual exercise for people who need to develop more self-confidence in their ability to love as Jesus loves.

Every morning, as you get out of bed, just say this little prayer: "Most Sacred Heart of Jesus, I give you this day. Help me to love as you love."

And each night, before you go to sleep, lying there in your comfortable bed, imagine that your head is on Jesus' chest and imagine you hear the beating of his heart. Reflect briefly on the day and try to remember the times you responded to people as Jesus would want you to respond, and the times you may have responded inappropriately for a Christian. Then, say this prayer: "Jesus, today you loved me and loved through me, maybe even in spite of myself. Thank you, Jesus. Help me to love everyone as you love and forgive me when I fail."

That's simple enough. If we do something like this every day, we will soon become more open to the love and presence of Jesus in our lives, and we will more often love as he loves.

PRAY, DECIDE, ACT

Reading

For we do not preach ourselves but Christ Jesus as Lord, and ourselves as your slaves for the sake of Jesus. For God, who said, "Let light shine out of darkness," has shone in our hearts, to bring to light the knowledge of the glory of God on the face of [Jesus] Christ. But we hold this treasure in earthen vessels, that the surpassing power may be of God and not from us. 2 Cor 4:5-7

Prayer

Father, help us to recognize you in our daily lives. Quicken our faith in Jesus through the power of the Holy Spirit that we may live a life of love in you and with you. Make our lives so attuned to your holy will and goodness that we are a living gospel to our children and godchildren. Teach us how to love unconditionally so that more people will come to know you through us. Amen.

Reflection

For Individuals or Groups

- I am most aware of God's presence in my life when . . .
- Reflect on the adults who had the greatest spiritual impact on you as a child. How did they affect you? What do their examples mean to you today?
- Have you ever sensed God's presence in a special way, had a moment when his peace seemed to fill you? Share this special moment with your friends.
- Think about your typical day. In what ways are you good news to others?
- As a god-family, what are two things we must accomplish to be good news for our children and godchildren?

For Parents

- Do you make time in your own day for Scripture and prayer?
- Do you share your faith with your children in a daily way?
- As a family, do you make a point of sharing your faith with your friends and neighbors?

For Godparents

- Is the heart of your Catholic faith a living relationship with Jesus? If so, how is it expressed? If not, explore why.
- Do you find it hard to share your faith with others? If so, what steps could you take to begin to share your faith more freely with others?
- Are there concrete ways in which you could share your life of faith with your godchild?

Action

1. We need to be more aware that the risen Jesus is alive in us. To help us grow as a god-family in that awareness and become more willing to share God with others, we will:

_____

_____

_____

2. We want to become a living gospel of love in all our relationships. To become more sensitive to the needs of others and of opportunities to love as Jesus loves, we will:

_____

_____

_____

3. We realize that love is the greatest power on earth. Love doesn't just happen. We have to work at it. We will discuss ways in which to practice love for each other. After that discussion we will decide on two or three "signs" of love that will be constant in our relationship. Toward that end, we will do the following:

_____

_____

_____

4. As a means of growing in our relationship with Jesus, we will pray the following prayer together now and at select times in the future:

_____

_____

_____

Prayer

Lord Jesus, I confess my need for you. Please come into my heart in a new and powerful way. Forgive me and heal me, Lord. I accept you as the Lord of my life. Live in me, Jesus, and fill me with the power to love as you love. Transform my life into a little gospel of love so that in all my relationships I can be an avenue of your love and your healing power. Amen.

SUGGESTED READING

Hart, Thomas N., *The Art of Christian Listening*. New York, N.Y.: Paulist Press, 1980.

The author helps readers understand the importance of listening. Used as a text in formation programs for priests and laity, *The Art of Christian Listening* is academic without being too "heavy." Godparents and parents often find themselves in the role of "helpers." Helpers have to listen and understand both what people are saying and not saying.

Knight, David, *His Word: Letting It Take Root—and Bear Fruit—in Our Lives*. Cincinnati, OH: St. Anthony Messenger Press, 1986.

If you wonder why Jesus' Word (the gospel) fails in your life, Jesus himself gives us three reasons—and Father Knight outlines them in his usual simple, readable, applicable style. This book is for everyone and anyone who wants to grow in their understanding of the gospel and how to live it.

Libersat, Henry, *Do Whatever He Tells You: Finding Joy in Pleasing God*. Boston, MA: St. Paul Books and Media, 1990.

Father Michael Scanlan of the Franciscan University of Steubenville has said that this book "gives solid Catholic teaching a contemporary flavor consistent with proclaiming the good news." Other reviewers have said that the book has "clarity and enthusiasm" and that it is "a practical, down-to-earth overview of Catholic moral teachings."

McKenna, Sister Briege, *Miracles Do Happen*. Ann Arbor, MI: Servant Publications, 1987.

Sister Briege's book has become an international best-seller. It is filled with beautiful, humorous and inspiring stories of God's healing love through prayer and sacraments. It's major strength is a lively, honest faith and an openness to let God work in the reader's life. Sister Briege helps readers seek God's will, believe in the power of prayer, and center their lives in the Eucharist and in God's Word.

FIVE

Through the Eyes of a Child

Recent research confirms the central role of home and family for the faith of contemporary Catholics. Studies over the past two decades reveal that the role of the home in the faith growth of children far outweighs that of parochial schools or religious education classes. Children learn what Catholics believe, how Catholics are to live and pray primarily by growing up in homes where the adults are struggling to believe, to pray and live as good Catholics. "Growing Up Catholic—at Home!"
Carl J. Pfeifer and Dr. Jan Manternach
The Family Piece, Volume 5, Number 1
National Catholic Education Association

F EW PARENTS HAVE TIME TO PURSUE METHODS COURSES in religious education, and I am not at all sure they should. Faith is something that is "more caught than taught." As the above quotation from *The Family Piece* emphasizes, it is in the home that Catholics are formed. Part of formation is teaching, passing on correct information. In the home, formation happens through relationships—interaction between family members. It happens as the child observes his parents and other adult role models such as godparents and grandparents.

It is hard for adults, particularly parents, to see the world through the eyes of their children. Parents are protective, and rightly so. They have legitimate authority over their children. Sometimes, however, that protective spirit and that authority get in the way of hearing our children.

Two personal examples are in order.

When I was about twelve years old, there was an epidemic of polio in our country. Every time we heard the news on the radio (no television in our rural area back then), there was talk about more and more polio cases, and more and more deaths. I became deeply terrified of getting sick and dying.

I lived in fear of death, and I have to admit that I received precious little consolation from my parents or parish priests. My parents fretted over the epidemic as much as I did, and about all I can remember hearing from priests is that we must "always be ready" to go to God because we "never know when he will call us to stand before him for judgment."

I had questions as well. What kind of God sent disease on people, even helpless babies and children?

Experiencing that fear of polio helps me understand better how today's children fear the power of nuclear weapons in the hands of fickle and even evil human beings. I can listen better to their fears.

The second personal experience involved my own lack of parenting skills. As a young father, I unfortunately believed children were to be seen and not heard and speak only when spoken to. I believed my children should grow up in the image of their parents and grandparents. After all, I was their father, and I was telling them what to do and what not to do, bringing them up as Catholics, and teaching them right from wrong, and all the rest.

I did not understand the impact their own peers would have on them or the influence of modern media, especially television. I never understood that just telling them right from wrong was a far cry from teaching them right from wrong. I tried to shove religion down their throats.

I'm amazed they turned out as well as they all did. But I can't help wonder how much easier it could have been on all of us had I better understood the beautiful fact that, even as little children, they were individuals called to be themselves—called to be all they could be and to discover for themselves the wonders of their God and their world. Our family would have been greatly blessed. I could have been more like a loving father than an autocrat.

When all of our children were still at home, Peg and I became involved in Family Education Leadership Training. The program was designed to train lay people to serve as family leaders in their parishes. Unfortunately, I saw it all as a bugaboo—as an interference in our way of life and a rather artificial approach to family relationships.

Part of the content of the educational series was learning how to develop relationships and communicate with children and spouses. With the benefit of hindsight, I realize I rejected the ideas and the entire program because my own security was threatened. I thought I was in control of my family, my kids knew who was boss. I thought reward and punishment were the best communication (in love, of course) you could develop in the family. In my family, everyone knew where he or she stood.

What a waste! I learned fifteen years later what a wonderful opportunity I had thrown away.

I mention this personal experience only because there may

be other parents who have difficulty growing as effective parents because of work, worry, cultural or emotional barriers, and misconceptions about authority and roles in Christian families.

It would be wonderful if parishes could increase their efforts in aiding parents in their mission to establish solidly Christian homes whose vision is to make the world a better place and whose mission is to extend the Christian faith into the marketplace.

Godparents, too, would benefit from parish family life programs. Those programs should encourage active relationships between parents, godparents, and children.

FACTORS AFFECTING THE FAMILY
AS A FAITH COMMUNITY

What does it mean to say the family is a "faith community"? I recall that during the 1950s the family was called "the church in miniature" and in more recent church teachings the family is called "the domestic church."

We all know that for the church to be fully *church*, the bishop must be present to the faithful. It is through the office of this overseer, the bishop, that we receive the sacraments and the authentic preaching of the Word of God. Yet in the committed and faithful Catholic family, the bishop is truly present—at least in spirit—because believers, through faith, obedience, Eucharist, love, commitment, and the action of the Holy Spirit are united in heart, mind, and soul with the rest of the church presided over by their bishop.

In this sense the family is indeed "the church in miniature," or "the domestic church," living the gospel in a world which is too often antagonistic toward the Word of God.

Because this "domestic church" lives in the world, it is essential that parents and godparents understand how the world affects the family.

What goes on in the larger world has a lot more impact on people than we might at first believe. For example, let's look at the various responses of people to the threat of a nuclear holocaust. Some people, faced with the reality that humanity has the sufficient technology and stupidity to annihilate itself, develop a sense of responsibility and try to change the course of history through voting, demonstrating, writing, and otherwise trying to help form public conscience. Others, facing the same fears, decide it best to "eat, drink, and be merry, for tomorrow we may die." Still others use the world tensions as an excuse to cop out entirely and dive headfirst into the oblivion of drug addiction or alcoholism.

Good religious education and formation in the home will give adequate attention to this moral and political issue that is so prevalent in the minds of people today. Good religious education cannot ignore contemporary problems any more than good medicine can ignore epidemics of AIDS, or herpes, or influenza.

Among the other forces affecting children are unacceptable attitudes about violence, sexual morality, race relations, economics, and equality of the sexes. For example, it is difficult to teach children to respect everyone regardless of color or ethnic origin when others are terming racial groups "niggers," "honkies," and "spics." It is difficult for parents to teach children to abstain from sexual relations until marriage when rock and movie stars glorify promiscuity, and public officials urge children to use condoms so sex can be "safe." In the child's world, just as in the adult's, common and ordinary, everyday situations have direct bearing on personality and faith development.

It is difficult to hold up "dead" saints as models for contemporary lifestyles when the hottest heroes going are the Ninja Turtles or the New Kids on the Block or Madonna. These heroes call attention only to personal power, personal pleasure, and personal liberation from all constraints. Today's heroes take the law into their own hands, flaunt legitimate authority, and glorify the use of violence to overcome violence.

It seems that a certain temporary insanity infects each younger generation from the silly, booze-sipping flappers of the 1920s, to the screaming bobby-soxers of the 1940s, to the double jointed jitterbuggers and rockers of the 1950s, and to the drug-consuming flower children of the 1960s and so on.

We've survived Sinatra and Elvis. I guess we'll survive Madonna, Michael Jackson, and Rambo, too. But it is very difficult for parents to try to help children see through their fantasies to the deeper message of contemporary entertainment. The craze is sinister and diabolical, much too serious to be taken lightly, especially with all the false religions, such as the New Age, being touted in sitcoms and rock music without any interference of the American Civil Liberties Union, which is usually so alert to any encroachment of religion on the public conscience.

Peer pressure is a powerful influence. Parents and godparents need to exert their own positive pressure. As a young Catholic journalist in Louisiana, I wrote a series of articles on how parents offset peer pressure among their children. Several parents developed uniform rules for their children. Once these rules were established, the children could no longer say, "But Johnny's mommie lets him stay out until midnight" or "Everybody else is doing it." Now the parents could turn the tables on their children. Since all the parents were using the same rules, the parents could say in each household, "You have to be in by ten o'clock because I say so and because 'everybody else is doing it!'"

There is a positive way in which parents and godparents can help young people overcome unfavorable influences in modern society, particularly in entertainment and the peer fascination with those bad influences: get involved in the children's entertainment.

One man I know, in corresponding about godparenting, suggested that parents and godparents should "get involved in wholesome forms of entertainment." In the movie, "The Women of Brewster Place," a young black couple produces a modern version of Shakespeare's "A Midsummer-Night's Dream." It was the first time many of the ghetto residents had ever attended a play and the impact on them, in the movie, was positive.

My correspondent said that he chose to read to his children and they loved to have him read to them. He wrote to me saying, "My children and I have had hours of pure pleasure by reading a half hour (or more because they demand it) from the following: *Chronicles of Narnia*, by C.S. Lewis; the *Little House Books*, by Laura Ingalls Wilder; *Where the Red Fern Grows*, by Wilson Rawls; *Bridge to Terabithia*, by Katherine Patterson; all of Roald Dahl's charming and hilarious books; poetry by Shel Silverstein; annotated *Pilgrim's Progress*; annotated *Life of Corrie ten Boom*; annotated Greek myths by Homer."

Reading with his children in the evening, "created an atmosphere of intimacy, of laughter, of absorption in wonderful worlds of fantasy and fact. They replaced the TV and to this day, my boys, age 9 and 11, *beg* me to read at night to them."

This father follows up with a paragraph from the Bible, without comment unless his sons ask him a question.

Such a commitment to children is indeed a sacrifice, but as with all sacrifices, it has great rewards. One benefit is quality time with the children. They know they are important because special and regular time is saved just for them. Also they are introduced into the world of pictures by words which is far more stimulating to the imagination than the "boob tube."

This is just one idea to show what parents and godparents can do to help children grow both intellectually and spiritually—as well as in loving relationships. We see how parents and godparents can help children follow better rules of behavior and develop more healthy and inquisitive minds: 1) responsible adults uniting to provide a peer system of acceptable rules and regulations, and 2) the simple act of reading to children.

In various dioceses in the United States, youth ministers have effectively organized Peer Ministry, a program designed to help young people help one another embrace and live the gospel message. This is a creative way to address unhealthy peer pressure. Peer pressure is as natural as a sunrise. To try to remove children from their peers is to destroy any hope for trusting relationships between parents and children. The best approach is one like Peer Ministry in which existing relationships are brought into the light of the gospel and young people are challenged to live higher standards.

Youth ministers and vocation directors claim that young people respond to challenges and to any confidence placed in them to meet those challenges. Perhaps parents and godparents need to step up the challenges too and the confidence placed in young people.

Adults must realize that peer pressure and oppressive forces in contemporary society have more impact on most children than do family prayer and Sunday Mass. Family stability and peace, school work and relationships, the neighborhood in which we live, the life of the city or community, amd national and international developments are all a part of our children's lives as well as our own. We cannot continue to act as though the influence of the world will be overcome by what we *tell* children *about* God or religion.

The best way to *teach* Catholicism to children is to *live* Catholicism in the home and marketplace. We have to share life with children—our lives, with our fears and our faith, with our strengths and our needs. If parents and godparents easily turn to the Lord in prayer, if they put their ultimate faith in God and not in money or political powers, if they live with hope for humanity and celebrate their lives, faith, and hope at Mass and in family celebrations, children will more easily develop a healthier sense of what it means to be Catholic.

Here is the key to helping young Catholics grow in their faith: To embrace faith as a way of life and not as a set of doctrines, to enter into the life of Jesus and not just learn about him. If adult Catholics are living their faith, their very lives are a gospel, a religious education program, and the real presence of Jesus.

NURTURING THE ROOTS OF CHILDREN

Children must be treated as individuals who have their own precious lives, gifts, personalities, limitations, dreams, and disasters. Each child is a microcosm of all creation, a special little sign or word of God, an eternal promise that life goes on, a member of the entire human family, a part of the world, and a little world unto himself or herself.

Children need to be nourished with a sense of belonging and caring. Affection is important. They need to be loved and to learn to love. Some psychologists believe that young adolescents can learn to belong to a faith community by hearing and rehearing the history of that community.

Many parents and godparents can recall listening to their parents and grandparents tell the "story" of their families, how they came to America, how they survived the Great Depression, how the family became established in this or that community. My wife's grandmother had a great gift for telling her family's story. I spent many hours listening to her talk about how her husband proposed to her, about her children, her own parents, brothers and sisters, about the first automobile in rural south Louisiana, about hard times and faith and love and births and deaths. Through her stories, I became more and more a part of Peg's family. Today I can share with them their joys and sorrows, their memories and their hopes.

I remember, too, hearing my parents talk about how much the church meant to them. There was no doubt that God and church were at the center of their lives. There was Mass on Sundays and holy days, no meat on Friday, and Christmas and Easter were observed as family feasts with a spirit of gratitude to God and dependence on him that had a great impact on me as a child.

Children who know their family history can more easily identify and belong to that family. I myself am deeply moved by the story of my ancestors from L'Acadie (now Nova Scotia) who suffered exile by the British rather than accept the religion of the King of England. They were put on ships as they watched their farms being burned, and all their earthly goods were confiscated. They were deported to the Carolinas and Georgia. From there, they eventually made their way to Southwest Louisiana where the Cajun (corruption of Acadian), Catholic culture took root and to this day thrives. I am part of that story, and my personal faith is enriched by those roots.

My own parents and godparents never shared the Cajun story with me. Maybe they were not themselves aware of how we came to Louisiana. That would not be surprising since the Cajuns got scattered throughout southwest Louisiana and had no teachers. They lost the ability to read and write and had no history books. When education came to Louisiana, the French language and history were suppressed and "American" history and English were taught exclusively.

However, I did learn a lot about my family from my parents, godparents, and grandparents. In late evenings, both in Texas and in Louisiana, sitting around fireplaces or space heaters, my elders would talk about old times, about family relationships through birth and marriage, about the "Big Depression" or the "First War." They spoke about how their own parents and grandparents had met and married, how families had always supported each family member when they were in trouble.

As I sat on an adult lap—Mama's, Daddy's, Aunt Ida's or Nan's—and dozed comfortably, my head against this or that bosom, hearing their voices resonate within their chest cavities, I learned what it meant to be a Libersat, a Zeringue, a Thibodeaux, a Trahan, and a Boudreaux. Even at an early age, because of my elders, I developed a deep sense of belonging, of an enduring sense of security born of my family's longevity over several generations. I was part of something bigger than me, even bigger than Mama and Daddy, in the middle of something strong and warm and secure, something that was rooted in God, in faith, in hope for the good that was promised and would come.

Although my family did not speak about their religion very often, everything they did, their entire life story, was rooted in belief in God, "going to Mass" and "obeying the Commandments." Often adults in my family would utter exclamations such as "In God we trust" or "It's God's will" or "God will help us." God was no stranger in our family. Their "faith story" was best told by their lives.

I can think of no greater gift to the present younger generation than a sense of family history, a sense of security born of belonging to those who love you and of a faith rooted in the loving heart of God.

Faith stories, particularly as they are told or echoed by other adults as well as by the parents, can go a long way in giving children and teenagers the kind of faith identity they need to carry them successfully through various stages of growth and development, especially the stage in which they tend to ignore anything their parents have to say.

Faith stories in church should have the same impact. I remember when it was popular to celebrate the lives of various saints. I was always deeply affected by the courage and faith of the martyrs. They became my heroes.

Besides faith stories, acting as role models helps children grow. I remember my struggles as an older adolescent, and the wonderful fact that I had good adult role models during that time when I chose to ignore or question anything my parents had to say. It was a time of desiring and fearing independence, of experiencing new and demanding drives and passions, of restlessness and rejections, of desires for intimacy and solitude.

Older adolescents want to decide for themselves what they should believe in. They like to experiment a lot, and that is why these young people are so susceptible to cults, drug pushers, and sexual immorality. They may even try pagan religions for a while. To them, nothing is sacred just because their parents say so. It stymies parents to realize that their children will take as gospel what some rock star says while rejecting the loving counsel of family and parish priest.

I remember at that age that I always thought I could more "be myself" when I was with Nan Stella or two very special cousins, Bob and Ruth Broussard. In those two families, there was a lot of laughter and things to do. There was good communication, and lots of it, between parents and children. Parents and children could tease one another, and everyone enjoyed a good joke, even the one on whom it was played. I don't think Nan, Bob, and Ruth ever realized just how important they were to me in those special years.

Godparents, if they have a faithful and joyful approach to life, can help their godchildren through some very difficult times. Sometimes children and teenagers experience loneliness. At other times, they may experience alienation from authority figures such as parents and teachers. Godparents, if they have developed as close a relationship as possible with their godchildren, can prove to be valuable friends.

When children are lonely, they need someone to help them understand loneliness. With my only brother nine years older than I, and living in a rural community in which most youths had a lot of work to do at home, much of my young life was lonely.

Bob and Ruth—and Nan Stella in Texas—understood that loneliness and tried to fill in the gaps, helped me appreciate myself more so that when alone, I could be less lonely.

Also when my parents and I were upset with each other, they somehow found a way to let me know they understood without ever encouraging disobedience. Sometimes, Bob and Ruth would just chuckle and say, "Boy, you've got a problem don't you?" and then we would all laugh together. Knowing that someone else, especially an adult, understood my hurt and disappointment or anger meant a great deal to me then—as it does now.

Professional counselors know that listening to someone else is a very important part of therapy. Perhaps you, too, have experienced the relief and peace that comes from talking out your troubles with an empathetic person.

Godparents, if they are to serve both parents and godchildren, have to be good listeners and friends of both parents and children.

One final point. We need to emphasize the *good* in young people. Adolescents, while seemingly rebellious and without firm convictions about religion, may often show strong commitment to working with the poor, the elderly, and with younger children needing special help. Even when they commit themselves to those philosophies, ideologies, or "isms" which drive parents batty, they are learning the nuts and bolts of commitment. It is for us, parents and godparents, to provide open doors and open arms, outlets for all that good will, challenges to searching intellects.

Parents and godparents need the help of the church and local educators to understand what their children are experiencing and to learn how to respond to the challenges presented to the child.

If parents, godparents, and parish work together, we can help our children develop ownership for the faith which we hold so dear, the faith which will help them become all that their loving Father intended them to become. We have to help our children grow up Catholic at home, or chances are, they will never grow up Catholic at all.

PRAY, DECIDE, ACT

Reading

...(Parents), it is your role to "be there"—be there to encourage, be there to listen, and be there to speak honestly about our own faith. It is for you as parents to be sensitive for the right moments: to know when to question and to know when to give a "little space." No one has the answers to all the questions which individual adolescent searching believers raise. But one thing is sure: If you live your own faith honestly and if you are available to your young people, you will be a positive factor in the growth of your teenagers' faith in Jesus Christ. We have his word.

Edmund F. Gordon, *A Journey Together*
For Parents and Sponsors in the "Emmaus Road" Program
Our Sunday Visitor

Prayer

Father, sometimes I feel so small when I face my responsibilities to bring a strong faith into my home and workplace. Especially, Lord, it is hard to be a good parent and godparent. Help me to understand better how to live my faith and to share it with my children and godchildren. In Jesus' name. Amen.

Reflection

For Individuals or Groups

I love my children and godchildren. I want what is best

for them. I want to be a loving and strong influence in their lives.

There are at least two different ways of being a parent or godparent: 1) I can become so involved with everyday routine and become so overwhelmed with problems and responsibilities that I miss a lot of the beauty in our relationship. 2) I can manage my life in such a way that I will schedule special time to be with these children, to enjoy them, and let them enjoy me.

I realize that part of parenting and godparenting is having fun together, discovering together how each of us experiences wonder and beauty and truth.

- Am I managing things or do things manage me?
- In the last couple of weeks, how have I expressed my appreciation for the gifts, talents, personality of my children or godchildren?

For Parents and Godparents

Here are some of the ways in which parents and godparents can contribute to the growth of young people:

- Subscribe to the Disney Channel for one year;
- Buy a child a subscription to National Geographic's *World* magazine;
- Ask the godparents to take the child on an historic vacation tour of a part of the United States;
- Take advantage of a child's pleasure at receiving mail and write encouraging letters about good TV programs and school work, sharing stories from your childhood;
- Spend time with a child watching ants or bees working;
- Buy the children wholesome video tapes—helping them discover characters they might otherwise never discover, such as Bud Abbott and Lou Costello, Roy Rogers, Gene Autry, and the Dead End Kids;

• Write a letter to a teenage or adult godchild who has lapsed from the faith;

• Help a godchild, if appropriate and without embarrassment to anyone, with expenses for field trips or for college tuition;

• Help a godchild prepare for marriage, sharing stories about weddings and marriages important in family history;

• Take a fishing trip together, or go to sports events or theater or good, wholesome movies.

Action

1. We will take a more active part in helping our children and godchildren find better entertainment by:

_____

_____

_____

_____

2. To create better understanding of our goals for the children, as parents and godparents, we will:

_____

_____

_____

3. To strengthen us in our understanding of faith development in children, we will ask our parish to provide:

_____

_____

_____

4. One of the secrets to a happy and productive life is the ability to "stop to smell the flowers." To grow in our appreciation for life and in our ability to play, as adults we will:

_____

_____

_____

_____

Prayer

Mary, you are our mother. You had the awesome responsibility of caring for the Son of God. We know that our children are also God's sons and daughters. As the perfect mother, with St. Joseph the perfect father, Jesus had protection, formation, and education. With your help he learned to pray and to decide in favor of his Father's will. Help us, Mary, and you, too, St. Joseph, with your prayers. Amen.

SUGGESTED READING

Gallagher, Rosemary, and Trenchard, John, C.SS.R., *Your Baby's Baptism*. Liguori, MO: Liguorian Publications, 1985.

This is a wonderful book (magazine size, complete with pictures) that helps parents understand better what happens when their baby is baptized. It is used by many parishes, along with a *videotape by the same name*, also available from Liguori.

Ghezzi, Bert, *Keeping Your Kids Catholic: It May Seem Impossible But It Can Be Done*. Ann Arbor, MI: Servant Publications, 1989.

Today, when so many secular influences are making it hard for children (and their parents and godparents) to embrace their faith, this book is a God-send. Mr. Ghezzi again shows his ability to go to the heart of a problem and seek for its solution in the heart and mind of God, all with a believable, down-to-earth involvement with life as it is truly experienced.

SIX

How to Belong to God and Each Other

I will deliver them from all their sins of apostasy, and cleanse them so that they may be my people and I may be their God. . . . I will make with them a covenant of peace; it shall be an everlasting covenant with them, and I will multiply them, and put my sanctuary among them forever. My dwelling shall be with them; I will be their God, and they shall be my people.

Ezekiel 37:23b, 26-27

WHEN I WAS ABOUT TWELVE YEARS OLD, the men in our family and a visiting friend decided to go fishing. I was very excited and ran to the barn to get my fishing tackle. With rod and reel in hand, a straw hat on my head, I joined the men in our sitting room.

My father looked at me, took the rod and reel and said, "Mr. 'X' doesn't have a pole. He can use yours. Only the men are going fishing today."

I was excluded. I was reminded I was not yet fully a man. I was devastated. Mr. "X" tried to dissuade my father because he saw how hurt I was, but my father was adamant: This fishing trip was for men only.

115

I still feel a deep sadness when I recall that incident. It wasn't missing the fishing trip that hurts. It was being excluded.

If we are true to our nature, we yearn to belong. Belonging is a basic, natural need. Even men who are "rugged individuals" want to gather at the pub on Fridays or Saturdays, form camping or fishing parties, or belong to a sports league.

Women also congregate with their peers, in groups dedicated to everything from sports to fashion, to charities and self-development, to business and professions.

Men and women—couples dating and married couples— tend to congregate with other couples. There is a natural, inborn need and desire to form relationships.

THE POWER OF RELATIONSHIPS

In spite of this great and natural need to form meaningful, supportive friendships, many relationships in society today are shallow, based on mutual self-gratification or economic and political needs.

Poor, desperate teenagers try to find intimacy through premature and sinful sexual relations. Adults forget that their sexuality is only one expression of their maturity, responsibility, and love.

Husbands treat their wives like housekeepers and convenient, cheap sexual partners. Women have become so dazzled by the promises of false liberation that they fail to appreciate what it means to be fully feminine, loving a man who is fully masculine.

Parents fail to be the kind of parents who see spiritual formation as the key to developing healthy children.

Employers and employees use others for their own selfish purposes, and see work only as a means to money rather than a means to personal and social fulfillment.

There are millions of cheap, harmful relationships in society today. Young people are not prepared well for marriage. I'd venture to say that eighty percent of young couples preparing for the sacrament of matrimony are people who have never made a personal commitment to Jesus Christ.

Many young couples live together before marriage. I've talked to them. They say that they can't afford to get married right now, although they truly love one another. I always respond, "You're living together right now. How would being married be more costly? You say you love one another. If that is true, why can't you make a lasting commitment which, finally, is the only proof of unconditional love?"

I am convinced that Christians, and especially Catholics, with the new emphasis on evangelization and community, can change society from within. We simply have to practice what we preach. If Christians truly believe that God lives in them, they will never be satisfied with relationships built on abuse, shallowness, and selfishness.

If Catholics take seriously their roles as parents and godparents, their families will become healthy and strong cells of society. Parents, godparents, and children can produce a model of family life that will appeal to millions of people who long for holy, loving relationships. A strong family, in the midst of such brokenness as we witness today, is a gospel of love and a reason to hope.

Christians bring to the marketplace that sense of reverence for each human being, that love, which makes them live for the sake of others. When entire Christian families have this God-inspired vision, the good is multiplied beyond the value of combined individual witness. A Christian community or family gives witness to the "workability" of love, grace, and commitment. This is something no individual can do alone, but only in relationship. This witness is something our world and the church sorely need.

Husbands, wives, parents, children, godparents, and relatives all benefit from good, faith-filled, and loving relationships, and so do all persons who come in contact with that loving family.

Christian friendships also have great healing and evangelizing power. Christian friends experience joy when they are together. When a Christian hears a friend's voice, his face lights up and glows with happiness. Sometimes, especially among the very young, Christians will jump with joy when they hear a friend's voice, perhaps in the same way John the Baptizer leapt in his mother's womb when Mary, pregnant with Jesus, approached.

I have only a few very good friends. One friend, in particular, is honest almost to a fault, always thinking and challenging himself and others. We disagree strongly on several different things in the church, but there is never any real anger or disappointment. Our relationship is built on mutual love and respect. He puts up with my ill temper, and I put up with his on certain days. It is a friendship that, like peace, surpasses understanding.

We come from two different worlds, he, from a New York business; I, from a Louisiana farm and later from Catholic journalism. He is about twenty years older and had the pleasure of early retirement, enabling him to stay home and help his wife rear their children. I am a working man and seem destined to continue working beyond retirement age, health permitting.

When I hear this friend's voice, I am always filled with a certain sense of peace and security. We are so comfortable together that our relationship spills over and touches others, such as waiters and waitresses in restaurants, mutual friends, and coworkers in the Lord's vineyard.

Actually, when I think of any or all of my close friends, I feel security, warmth, love, and contentment. I also feel blessed that God has given me such companions.

What makes these friendships special? We have a sure conviction that God is in us and loves us. We personally *know* God rather than only knowing *about* him.

Heaven is a mystery, but it is a place of security where nothing and no one can make you feel threatened and unloved. My friendships, rooted in faith, are experiences of heaven. With these friends, my wife and children are the closest of those friends, I never feel insecure or unloved.

Imagine what would happen to your home, your workplace, your neighborhood, or your parish if such love existed! You and your family and friends can begin to strengthen your relationships through consciously sharing faith and praying for growth in love.

"See how those Christians love one another!" That is how people are supposed to know us, by the way we love, by the depth of our love, by the spiritual power of our love.

Yet Americans shy away from sharing their faith. Religion is a "private" matter, they say. Because of this notion of "privacy," it is almost impossible to keep people's minds on God's will and power in the work-a-day world.

However, a vibrant, living faith cannot be smothered in the contempt society holds for God, the church, and religion. True faith is a brilliant light that shows up the danger and horror of a society which has put God on a leash.

If families and god-families have such a faith, they become a life of Christian witness and ministry in the world, they spread the faith, and they become aware of saving their own immortal souls.

WHERE DO WE BEGIN?

If we want to develop Christian relationships that have the power to transform the world, where do we begin? The first step is to overcome that tendency toward "rugged individualism" in ourselves.

While preparing for this final chapter of *Godparents*, I experienced a series of serious professional problems. Suffering from depression didn't help at all. The more I tried to solve the problems, the bigger the problems grew.

Honestly, I had become too busy to pray. I was not in proper relationship with God or anybody else. I was short-tempered, tired too easily, and subconsciously was looking for sympathy and a miraculous solution to all my problems.

One night I was so keyed up I couldn't sleep. At two in the morning, I got up from bed and decided to get ahead of the game by doing morning prayer right then.

I picked up the breviary and opened it to the Office of Readings for that particular day. The first line that caught my eye declared: "Surrender to God, and he will do everything for you."

Needless to say, I stayed with that one line for quite some time. Two or three days later, the Office of Readings contained a sermon by John Chrysostom, a saint who had a magnificent gift of preaching. John explained that sheep, and not wolves, receive the Shepherd's care. In being sheep, we naturally follow in the footsteps of the Shepherd. When we become wolves—people who struggle on their own to get what we need or want, sometimes at the expense of others— we put ourselves at odds with the Shepherd. We leave his care. Yet we must be in relationship, first with God, then with others, if we wish to be productive.

It is so hard to try to believe in a God whom we cannot see and so many of us never feel or experience. It is hard to form a relationship with an invisible person. As children we learn that God is everywhere. We never fully understand that mystery because we cannot be everywhere. We are limited by time and space.

Maybe this little example will help. On the Feast of the Immaculate Conception, one of our parish priests shared this insight in his homily. Speaking to children, trying to help them understand how God can be everywhere, he said:

Once, a little baby deer, a fawn, went up to his mother and asked, "Mama, what is this thing called air? I hear everyone talking about air but I don't know what it is." Mama Deer answered, "Why air is everywhere. It's all around you, it's in you. It gives you life."

Baby Deer still did not understand, so Mama Deer said, "Look, go to the lake and stick your head under the water and then you will know what air is."

What murky waters we enter when we lose our relationship to God! It is only when we surrender to his presence that life again becomes a place to breathe freely without anxiousness.

God is very near indeed, in his Word, his own Son who becomes our food in the Eucharist. He is in every sunrise and sunset, in babies' smiles and the embraces of loved ones. He is in the priest who raises his hand in absolution and in the lay person who works hard to love everyone in his or her workplace. Our God is among the stars and in our hearts, in the United Nations and in city council meetings, in construction crews and in operating rooms, in the executive offices of hotels and in the family kitchen.

God is in you and in me. He is in us, making us one, transforming us through the power of his Holy Spirit.

When it comes to growing in faith and in forming good Christian relationships, God has done most of the "work" for us. We have only to accept—perhaps with fear, doubt, or skepticism—the gift of life, forgiveness, and love he has already handed us on a silver platter.

Far too often, we think of our children's baptism more than we do of our own. However, our baptisms made us daughters and sons of God, heirs to God's kingdom, *co-heirs with Christ*. We are called to a true and deep faith in Jesus. If we have that kind of faith, we can love as Jesus loved, and that is a very demanding love. First, however, we must surrender to God.

HOW CHRISTIANS ACT

St. Paul, while in prison, reflected on the meaning of living in Christ, of being Christian, and of developing Christian relationships. In his letter to the Colossians, he tells us:

> You were buried with him in baptism, in which you were also raised with him through faith in the power of God, who raised him from the dead. And even when you were dead [in] transgressions and the uncircumcision of your flesh, he brought you to life along with him, having forgiven us all our transgressions; obliterating the bond against us, with its legal claims, which was opposed to us,

he also removed it from our midst, nailing it to the cross; despoiling the principalities and the powers, he made a public spectacle of them, leading them away in triumph by it. **Col 2:12-15**

Isn't that a magnificent message? Look at the promise and joy. We have been raised with Christ. We were loved and given new life even while we were in sin. He loved us and sent Jesus to redeem us, to lead us back to him, to experience victory over sin because those very sins have been crucified with Jesus on the cross. God has made a mockery of the devil and all his false promises and all his little demon helpers. He has led them off into captivity.

We learn from Acts and from John's Gospel that Jesus sends us his Holy Spirit to instruct us in the ways of God, to form us into a loving community, to enflame us with God's love. One gift given us by the Holy Spirit is piety, or as I call it, the gift of love or the gift of right relationship. It is that gift which, I believe, we need in order to form Christian relationships. If I am filled with God's love, I realize he loves everyone, and if God loves everyone, who am I to show favorites? Am I smarter than God? Do I know something about Tim or Alice or Father Smith or Dr. Jones that God does not know?

Christian relationships are possible only through the power of the Holy Spirit, who is himself love. Look what Paul demands of us:

Put to death, then, the parts of you that are earthly: immorality, impurity, passion, evil desire, and that greed that is idolatry....But now you must put them all away: anger, fury, malice, slander, and obscene language out of your mouths. Stop lying to one another....

Put on then, as God's chosen ones, holy and beloved, heartfelt compassion, kindness, humility, gentleness, and

patience, bearing with one another and forgiving one another, if one has a grievance against another; as the Lord
has forgiven you, so must you also do. And over all these
put on love, that is, the bond of perfection. Col 3:5, 8-9, 12-14

Bear with one another. Forgive. Be patient.

None of these are possible without the grace of God's
Holy Spirit, but with the Spirit comes the strength to live a
life of peace in Christ, a life that will give us sheer joy, even
in the middle of great trials and adversity.

Think of your relationships with your children, godchildren, spouse, and parents. Think of the times when you felt
distance growing in those relationships. What caused the
hurt? What prolonged the tension and the ill-will, the anger
and resentment? What could you have done, or what can
you do even now, that would fulfill Paul's pastoral direction,
that would help heal strained or broken relationships?

Once I attended a huge state-wide conference in Florida.
As one of the speakers, I sat on the stage. At the close of the
conference, during the final prayer and hymn, I noticed a
family crying and hugging one another in the first rows in
the auditorium. The father and the sons were big men, each
more than six feet tall and weighing more than two hundred
pounds. Yet, here they were, macho and all, hugging, crying,
and laughing, pounding one another on the back. I could
read their lips. They were saying, "I'm sorry" and "I love
you" and "Please forgive me."

Throughout that auditorium families were being recon-
ciled, individuals were feeling God's presence and love. The
Holy Spirit was working a mighty work, and the power of
God was manifest.

That can happen right in your own home, with your own
family and god-family.

God does not intend that we suffer bitterness and resentment, that marriages fail, that families be broken, that relatives and friends fall out and become estranged. No. God intends that we live in love, peace, and harmony, that we share his power over evil and his power for creative good. We are made in his image, not Satan's. We are his children, not Satan's. We are children of light, not darkness. We are his people, the sheep of his flock, not the playthings of the devil.

In God, we are powerful, not powerless. In God, we find order, not chaos. In him we find wisdom, not anxiety.

BEING AWARE OF GOD'S PRESENCE

Here are five things we can do to become more aware of God's presence in our lives, things we can do that will help us make God the center of our lives and the source of our peace and power.

1. Stop, look, listen. Don't take life or people for granted. As you drive familiar streets each day, make yourself see your neighborhood, city, state. Really see the growing children, trees and flowers, the changing seasons, the shadows, the lawns, the colors, the birds, the cars. Be conscious of what is around you. Listen to the sounds—the barking of dogs, shouts of children, squealing of tires, singing of birds. All these sights, sounds, smells, people, and things are gifts from God. Feel his presence in them.

Most importantly, don't take your own family for granted. Each day try to see and hear your spouse, children, godparents, and godchildren. God is present in them, for you; and present in you, for them.

2. Make your life a prayer. Each morning offer to God your entire day with all its joys and sorrows, work and play. Train yourself to be conscious of his presence so that throughout the day, it will be easier for you to remember he is with you even when things go wrong. In the evening at bedtime spend a few moments reviewing the day. "Were there moments in which I acted as though he were not with me?" Replay those events in your mind. Try to pinpoint the moment you began to act like a wolf rather than a sheep.

Concentrate especially and specifically on family relationships and how you responded to your loved ones that day.

3. Spend time each day in formal prayer. Your life cannot be a prayer if you are not formally praying. Have a special time and a special place reserved for just you and God. At the same time, families must spend time praying together. Family prayer will be enriched to the degree each member spends time in personal, formal prayer.

4. Read and follow God's Word. Get yourself a Bible. Read it and obey it. God's Word is comforting, instructional, challenging, soothing, edifying, corrective, admonishing, encouraging, life-giving, and healing. Don't be a stranger to the very Word from which your faith flows and to which your life is moving from day to day. This is essential to being Catholic.

I recommend that individuals, families, and god-families spend time each week reflecting on the coming Sunday's Scriptures, praying over them and trying to apply them to daily life. Let each family member share what the Scripture message means to him or her personally and to the family as a whole.

When Sunday comes, the proclamation of God's Word and the homily will be more meaningful and fruitful. Get the list of readings from the church bulletin or the missalette, but read them in the Bible. I recommend the *New American Bible*, since this translation is used in the liturgy.

5. Spend time together. *No job, no church activity,* is more important than loving relationships in the home. In a fall issue of *The Wall Street Journal* in 1990, a story was run about lay-offs of top executives on Wall Street. One man said he had so dedicated himself to his job, *for his family's sake,* that he never had a chance to eat breakfast with his wife. Such executives, the story said, were habitually awakened at two or three in the morning by their bosses or clients and had to be ready to leave town on a business trip any time of day or night, regardless of family or other responsibilities.

Admittedly, that is an extreme case, but all of us can fall victim to doing things *for the family's sake* while we neglect the family. If we honestly examined our own consciences, we may find our workaholism is rooted in selfishness, and love of power, money, and prestige rather than love of family. Make time together, plenty of time, and quality time at that.

THE CALL TO MISSION

I believe that god-families are perhaps the church's greatest untapped source of evangelistic power in the home and community. We have to appreciate our Christian mission. By simply living and loving every day in the name of Jesus and trusting him to fill us with the wisdom of his Spirit, we will become effective Christians. If we see daily life as our vocation, our call from God, either married or single, priest, religious or lay, we will fulfill our role in the world.

I am convinced that if we take godparenting more seriously and begin to develop god-families in our parishes, the church will experience ever greater success in its efforts to strengthen family life, our young people, and the church in the modern world.

Parents and godparents, praying and loving together, can help Christian families become islands of love and hope in a world that so often seems to be a sea of confusion and, often, despair.

God has visited his people.
God has called his people.
God has sent his people.
You are that people.

Pray, Decide, Act

Reading

When the day of Pentecost came it found them gathered in one place. Suddenly from up in the sky there came a noise like a strong driving wind which was heard all through the house where they were seated. Tongues as of fire appeared, which parted and came to rest on each of them. All were filled with the Holy Spirit. They began to express themselves in foreign tongues and make bold proclamation as the Spirit prompted them. Acts 2:1-4

Prayer

Come, Holy Spirit. Fill our hearts. Set us on fire with love for God. Fill our minds with truth, especially the truth that we are equipped by you to do what God asks us to do. Renew us and all our relationships just as you renewed the failing spirits of the disciples on that first Pentecost. Give us the wisdom, strength, and self-confidence we need, Holy Spirit, to do well what God asks us to do. In Jesus' name, Amen.

Reflection

For Individuals or Groups

- I want all my relationships to be renewed and strengthened. I don't want to be satisfied with shallow and superficial relationships. I don't want to fall victim to materialism or greed or ambition.
- Which relationships in my life are most affected by superficial concerns: on the job? at home? in the parish?
- How did these relationships begin? How did they fail to grow?
- I really want to believe that God can change my life, give me a lively faith and more self-confidence in sharing my faith with others in family, god-family, and workplace.
- If I find it hard to believe that God is with me and empowers me to fulfill my calling, why is that so?
- Have I been open to the transforming grace and power of the Holy Spirit? How can I become more open?

For Parents

- Do I make time for God and others in my day?
- As a family, do we take the time to pray, share, and appreciate life with each other?
- How are we going to involve our children's godparents in the life of our family?

For Godparents

- Are relationships important to my life of faith? If so, which ones?
- How can I develop stronger relationships to support my life in Christ?
- Where do my relationships with members of my god-family fit into my life of faith? How can I make these relationships a vital part of my life?

_____

Action

1. To become more aware of the power of the Holy Spirit in our lives, we will:

_____

_____

_____

_____

2. To begin to strengthen relationships in our lives, we will:

_____

_____

3. Marilyn Norquist-Gustin, in *The Beatitudes, Jesus' Pattern for a Happy Life,* provides us with deep insights into the Christian life. Her little book is well worth reading by parents, godparents, and by teenagers. The beatitudes, after all, were given us by Jesus himself. They are his challenge, his call. If we live them, we will be living as Jesus lived.

Parents and godparents may want to reflect together on the beatitudes. Perhaps they could take one beatitude a week to study and reflect on, applying it to life at home and on the job and to all relationships.

You'll find the beatitudes in Matthew's Gospel, 5:1-12.

Prayer

Father, to celebrate our unity and love, we now join hands and pray, slowly and intently, the prayer Jesus taught us to pray:

Our Father, who art in heaven, hallowed be thy name. Thy kingdom come. Thy will be done, on earth as it is in heaven. Give us this day our daily bread, and forgive us our trespasses as we forgive those who trespass against us, and lead us not into temptation, but deliver us from evil. Amen.

And now, my dear friends, may Almighty God bless you, the Father, Son, and Holy Spirit.

Go in peace, to love and serve the Lord, to establish God's reign in your hearts, families, and in the world which God loves so very much.

Amen! Alleluia!

SUGGESTED READINGS

Angelica, Mother M., *Mother Angelica's Answers, Not Promises: Straightforward Solutions to Life's Puzzling Problems.* New York, N.Y.: Harper & Row, 1987.

This is a book rooted deeply in both Scripture and Tradition, written in the nitty-gritty style in which this delightful Franciscan cloistered nun teaches. Founder of Eternal Word Television Network in Birmingham, Alabama, Mother Angelica has produced a book which helps Catholics rediscover the wealth of Catholic spirituality—a boon for anyone seeking to grow and live as a Catholic.

Norquist-Gustin, Marilyn, *The Beatitudes: Jesus' Pattern for a Happy Life.* Liguori, MO: Liguorian Publications, 1981.

Here is a handbook on how to live the beatitudes. Marilyn Norquist-Gustin provides practical ways in which to grow in the virtues Jesus outlined in his famous sermon on the mount. Easy to read, this book should be a great help to parents and godparents who want practical ways to help their god-family grow in love and holiness.

Nouwen, Henri J.M., *Reaching Out: The Three Movements of the Spiritual Life.* Garden City, N.Y.: Doubleday and Company, Inc., 1975.

This is a special book which helps contemporary Christians stand against the forces which alienate people, driving them into loneliness, making them hostile, and encouraging time to live lives of illusion. A real help for people who care for themselves and others.

Survey on Godparenting

Please answer as many of the following questions as possible.

I. Your preparation and experience in godparenting.

A. Do you feel you had adequate preparation to be a good godparent? Circle one.

Yes   No

B. What did the local parish offer in terms of preparation for baptism?

For parents of the child?

_____

_____

For the godparents?

_____

_____

C. On a scale of 1 to 10, with 10 being absolutely great, how do you feel you rate as a godparent? Circle one.

    1   2   3   4   5   6   7   8   9   10

D. Have you ever felt any guilt or fear in godparenting, and if so, why?

        Yes   No

Explain

_____

_____

_____

E. Which of the following words best describes your understanding of what a godparent should be? Circle one.

    good example;   guide;   mentor;   friend;

  teacher;   substitute parent;   protector of the faith

F. Godparenting can be rewarding and fun! Please give an example, if you can, of the most fun or joy you've experienced as a godparent:

_____

_____

_____

_____

_____

II. The art of godparenting.

A. In what ways have you and the parents of your godchild celebrated and grown in your relationship with each other?

_____

_____

_____

_____

_____

B. I see my godchild... Circle one

　　1. Frequently   (once a week)
　　2. Occasionally   (once a month)
　　3. Rarely   (once a year)
　　4. Hardly ever.

C. How have you "stayed in touch" with your godchild? Regularly or on special occasions? Greeting cards or personal letters or both?

_____

_____

_____

_____

III. Growing with the godchild.

A. Have you had a "good experience" in helping your godchild grow in faith and develop a relationship with God? If so, please describe what you have done to help this along:

_____

_____

_____

_____

B. Whether or not you consider yourself a "very successful" godparent, please give us the benefit of your hindsight.

1. What would you do differently today with a new godchild in establishing a solid, faith-filled relationship?

_____

_____

_____

_____

2. What help would you want from the child's parents in becoming more effective in godparenting?

_____

_____

_____

_____

3. What would you expect from the local parish in helping you become a more effective godparent?

_____

_____

_____

_____

4. What can be done to make prayer part of the relationship of parents, godparents, and godchild?

_____

_____

_____

_____

C. What challenged you most in dealing with your teenage godchildren? How did you meet the challenge?

_____

_____

_____

_____

_____

IV. Putting flesh on the theory

A. Rate your agreement with each of the following statements:

1. Parents and godparents should have clear "ground rules" for dialogue and discussing tough issues. Circle one

Strongly agree,   Agree,   Disagree,   Strongly disagree

2. Parents and godparents should share the responsibility for the rearing of the child, particularly in faith development. Circle one.

Strongly agree,   Agree,   Disagree,   Strongly disagree

3. Local parishes should do more to help parents and godparents understand their roles and live up to the responsibilities they assume. Circle one.

Strongly agree,   Agree,   Disagree,   Strongly disagree

B. Would you kindly share with us the story about the warmest, funniest, or most challenging moment(s) in your experience as a godparent? Please try to do it in two hundred words or less.

_____

_____

_____

_____

_____

_____

_____

_____

_____

_____

_____

_____

_____

_____

_____

_____